Damn Bunch of Cripples

Damn Bunch of Cripples

◆

My Politically Incorrect Education in Disability Awareness

Lew Shaver

iUniverse, Inc.
New York Lincoln Shanghai

Damn Bunch of Cripples
My Politically Incorrect Education in Disability Awareness

iUniverse, Inc.

For information address:
iUniverse, Inc.
2021 Pine Lake Road, Suite 100
Lincoln, NE 68512
www.iuniverse.com

ISBN: 0-595-29254-2

Printed in the United States of America

To my mom and dad, Eva and Gerald, my sister, Jeane, my children, Lynette and Derek and my wife, Judy.

Contents

Acknowledgements

There are so many wonderful people in my life who have assisted, supported, and challenged me along the way. Space limitations prevent me from recounting and/ or acknowledging every one of them.

My family ranks number one.

Thanks to the great group of student-athletes and the student-managers who endured and who shared such a unique experience. And to all the individuals who were my mentors, my colleagues and my friends. I can only thank all of you with these words.

You deserve all my thanks and love and more.

Introduction

I was sitting in a small upstairs bedroom that was being converted to a personal den attempting to write this personal account of my education in disability awareness. I was sitting and paging through some old scrapbooks when the realization hit me, "I did it. I retired." And I'm sitting here thinking about all the years that have gone. I smiled a bit, remembering my thoughts as a child and as a young man about people that were retired, "Damn, they are old."

I was especially struck by the thought that here I set, just like some of the old, and I now mean old movies where the hero is remembering his life story and then the actual flashback as that life is recreated on the screen. One movie in particular, starring James Cagney, *The Gallent Hours,* came to mind. Cagney was playing the role of "Bull" Halsey on his retirement from the Navy after World War II. He was sitting in his office aboard a ship waiting to attend his retirement ceremony and his thoughts wandered back to a specific experience, the hours surrounding his taking command of the Guadalcanal Operation during the early months of the war.

Wow, I thought, it really does happen. I have become they. All the old people that as a kid I thought were really old and really weird were now me. I could always remember my dad introducing me to old buddies and how they always spouted the same thing, about how I had grown and how they knew me when I was only this high, indicating my height by their hand somewhere down around their knee. It was always the same and I can remember how I thought they were all so full of shit. Of course there were also the old women who would grab and pull me into their boobs which were big, I mean big, smothering big, and exclaiming how cute they remembered I was and what a fine young man I was growing up to be. And my dad would stand there glowing, so damn proud of his little prodigy, and me hating every encounter.

At least I understood that the alternative stunk. Thank God I had reached this point in my life. Many don't. But now that I was at this point in life, I was thankful but also a bit scared. Whereas sixty plus was ancient at one time and as the old saying goes, "with one foot in the grave and the other on a banana peeling", here I am. Thoughts such as how many more years do I really have and how is my health going to be were more than just mental gymnastics any more. It was now,

1

and it was the reality. And I sat, doing and thinking the same thoughts and doing the same things I made fun of earlier.

After almost forty years of teaching and coaching, with a divorce along the way, and an alcoholic treatment experience included, I had retired. If someone would have suggested that cute little Lew Shaver would become divorced or an alcoholic, I would have had a good laugh. After all, I taught in the field of health education and comically, maybe not a good word, about drugs. I smiled at this thought and now realize I really did not have a clue. My God, the divorce was some twelve years ago and the alcoholic episode was now ten. Time flies when you're having fun, right? I was one of the fortunate ones. I met a wonderful person. After months of desperation and despair, for everyone involved, I begin to 'get it.' This is a story unto itself and heavens only knows there are thousands and thousands of such stories, but this is not this story. It's a part of it. And to say I was fortunate would not begin to tell the entire story. I met, as I said a wonderful woman, Judy, remarried and life is good, very good.

Sure, I could always tell others what to do. Hell I was good at that. Aren't we all? Some just better than others, but in retrospect, I had no clue.

One very real issue was how to deal with the present climate of political correctness. My decision was to tell the stories as I remember them, in the language as I remember. To do different in my opinion would change and compromise the actual experience. It would sanitize the essence of the moment, thought, or action. This would radically change and lessen the integrity. I tried hard to keep in mind my own foibles and imperfections. To describe situations and individuals, as I personally perceived them was troubling, as I did not want to embarrass anyone. I struggled with this and decided that to be less than honest, first with myself and second with those that were involved would perhaps become a contrivance written to please others. I'm not sure any of them need, nor want me, to feel like I have to take care of their feelings. As a youngster, growing up, I played a lot of pickup baseball games. Whoever owned the ball made up the rules; well, this is my ball.

There are two other issues I will address.

The first involves my language. I have already shared that the stories will be as close to what I can recall. My language is colorful. This is probably an understatement. Many people find it offensive and vulgar. It is a part of me, a very real part. I do not want to turn people off when I am trying to present this. What is said in the locker rooms and at practices and during games is almost privileged conversation. And yet it is public domain. Some of my players and teams have been sworn to secrecy about half times and other of my verbal outbursts. This is not an attempt to defend such oration. It happened. I will attempt to deal with this issue as best I can without the sanitization effect totally changing the particular story or moment. Some people have suggested I not worry about this, but in all honesty, I want to say something. I still work on this issue every day and suspect I will until they throw dirt in my face. One player put it rather well, "Hell coach, if you didn't say Goddamit every once in a while, we would have thought you were sick or we wouldn't have known what you were saying."

The second issue involves a certain amount of medical involvement to my experience. Some of it sure is boring but some of it is vital, to a point of being life and death. Sometimes, it is tough to determine the importance. I certainly did not need to have the knowledge of say a neurologist or a brain surgeon. I will try to share what I think might be important to the experience. This is my perception, my narrative.

1

Beginnings

Most of us have had defining moments or have made significant decisions that certainly change our lives. This is a bit of history of a particular decision that was momentous for me, a little Southern Illinois boy moving to Marshall, Minnesota. I had to look hard on a map to be sure where Minnesota was and even harder to find Marshall. My concept of the area was somewhat akin to a land of 'Nanook of the North,' with frozen tundra reminiscent of Siberia. Hey, what did I know! The uniqueness of the experience lies in the fact I became involved as a coach in wheelchair sports.

For over twenty-five years, a group of young people and I shared the thrill of victory and the agony of defeat. We shared the trials and tribulations, the joys and heartaches associated with completion at the intercollegiate level.

I arrived at Southwest Minnesota State College in the fall of 1969 at age thirty-two. I had accepted a teaching position at SMSC (later to be renamed Southwest State University—SSU and recently renamed Southwest Minnesota State University—SMSU). My appointment was as a health educator in the department of health and physical education.

My life and teaching background had been spent in Southern Illinois. I grew up in Roxana, a very small town of some 2,000 souls across the Mississippi River from St. Louis, Missouri. Beside myself, my family included my Mom and Dad, Eva and Gerald, and a sister, two years younger than me, Jeane. Jeane could out run, out jump any boy in the neighborhood and could 'beat the snot' out of her older brother. I think I began to catch up with her somewhere around age thirty, if I have ever caught her!

The Missouri River joins the Mississippi in this area and the Ohio River joins just south, some two hundred miles or so. In addition, the Illinois River joins this area just twenty miles north. There were lots of water, skeeters, snakes, and humidity. I swear there were days when the humidity was 100%, and it wasn't raining! The Illinois side was a bedroom community for St. Louis and was highly industrialized with steel mills and oil refineries. As a matter of fact, Roxana sat in the middle of three refineries, including Shell Oil and Standard Oil. These were the days before pollution awareness, and the air was filled with smoke and always smelled of gasoline and oil. The sky was gray. The surrounding communities, which ran into one another for miles, always referred to Roxana as 'Stinkyville.' My dad used to say, "Hell, that's money you smell." It meant jobs. That's why we had moved up into the area in 1941, when I was four years old, from even deeper south in Southern Illinois. My dad took a job at Shell Oil Refinery.

A blue collar area, shift work was just an accepted way of working as the plants were running twenty-four hours a day, 365 days a year. Later, my dad took a second job selling cars. We were poor I guess, but we never gave it a thought as I can recall. And the phrase 'lower socioeconomic' wasn't invented yet and probably would have angered us should someone have suggested we were part of it. We always had clean clothes, food on the table, a pair of school shoes and another play pair, so 'Little Lew' was OK. At the time I didn't realize that Shell Oil paid most of the taxes for the community which gave us good town services such as street maintenance, garbage pickup and so forth. I never gave it a thought that the high school nickname was 'The Shells' and our logo had an oil truck with refinery columns as the central theme. Hey, the town next door, Wood River, was called, 'The Oilers.' Think we weren't company towns?

As kids we spent the summers playing ball from sun up to sun down. My dad always made sure I had lots of sports equipment. He was a pretty good ball player himself and played on the town team. He was a catcher, so I inherited his old equipment. This made me valuable, as I was one of the few kids with catcher's equipment, which meant I became a catcher. I was the littlest one around, and I wound up behind the plate. The catcher's mitt was so big and hard that if I didn't smother the ball with my right hand as the ball hit the glove it would actually carom back towards the pitcher's mound. Many a time my hand would get there a bit early and play hell with my fingers. This was just part of being tough. If my dad could catch, that was good enough for me. Besides it pretty well assured me of a place to play. Dad used to call catcher's equipment, "Tools of ignorance." Like father, like son.

When we weren't playing ball we played bike tag all over town. Two people would be "it" and try to catch the rest of us. If you got tagged, you joined in the hunt until there was only one left. That one was the winner, of what I'm not sure. Tagging consisted to trying to touch someone, with any body part or with your bike, as you caught up to him or her. A neat idea, and I guess not the least bit on the simple side. We resorted to any means. Ramming was legal, or at least accepted. We did whatever worked! Remember, this was before helmets and all the safety consciousness of today. Poor bikes, we were always repairing them. It might not have been too bright, but it was one hell of a game. Of course, we modified our bikes. We replaced the handlebars with car steering wheels. We put baseball bubblegum cards in our spokes to sound like motors. Wonder what those cards would be worth today? We turned the handlebars in all directions and put different size wheels or made tandem bikes out of two. Necessity is the mother of invention, and did we invent.

Then, of course there were the handy-dandy BB guns, Daisy, had lever action, just like Roy Rogers' used. Hell you couldn't be a kid in Roxana and not have a BB gun. They were great for shooting birds, streetlights (although I never participated in this hooliganism). It was amazing how many streetlights were replaced over the years. No sir, Momma Shaver's little cherub wouldn't do something like that. But what I did do, which was really stupid was to be in BB gun fights. Yep, right out of the old west, good guys against the bad guys. I went home with many a whelt on my body. Momma Shaver did not take too kindly to this. Believe it or not no one ever lost an eye. God takes care of dumb animals and dumb kids. We would also float bottles down drainage ditches and shoot the hell out of them, sinking them. One particular ditch ran along the Standard Oil property line. We would collect bottles out of trashcans, (we called it 'alley junking') and take them down to the ditch, throw them up stream and blast away. I suspect if you collected all the glass from that ditch the world wouldn't need any glass made for decades.

After high school I spent two years in the Army, graduated from college, and returned to Roxana to teach. I taught for two years as an elementary physical education specialist (which meant I taught at five different elementary schools using my car as a sporting goods store) plus five years as a high school health teacher. During this time, 1961–68, I also served as an assistant football and baseball coach. Sports had always been important in my life. In high school I played football, basketball and baseball and in college I played a year of varsity basketball. Coaching was a natural addition to my teaching responsibilities. In 1968, through a former professor, I had an opportunity to accept a fellowship to continue my education. I had finished my Master's Degree in 1965. I thought that my coaching career was coming to an end with this decision. Little did I know what was to be in my future. After a year of postgraduate work at Indiana State University, I accepted a teaching position at Southwest Minnesota State College in Marshall, Minnesota.

I interviewed in March of '69. I flew into Minneapolis-St. Paul, and on my 3 hour ride to Marshall saw nothing but snow. People put flags on their car antennas so they could be seen at corners and intersections. This blew my mind! I was in no way prepared for this. The tundra was for real. Highways were like tunnels with huge walls of snow. And God, it was cold! The people of the college and the town were great. I interviewed for two days. One particular person spent a good deal of time questioning me about a goose hunting area in Southern Illinois where he had hunted, and how he enjoyed it. We shared a few hunting stories, and as he walked away, I was informed I had just been interviewed by the Vice President. I was impressed. There was no attitude of administrative hierarchy, just great educators as far as I could tell. Despite the obvious weather drawbacks I took the position on the way back to the 'Twin Cities' airport and never looked back.

Southwest Minnesota State is described in its various recruiting publications as a four-year technical and liberal arts institution located in Marshall, Minnesota on the prairie of the southwest region of the state. It opened in 1967 on a 216-acre campus. Its unique feature is that it was architecturally conceived and designed to facilitate the movement of individuals with disabilities.

In February of 1974, *Sports Illustrated,* featured an article about the school's very successful swimming program "Big fish in a small pond," which described the school as having, "frustrations that have built up ever since the Minnesota legislature created Southwest to inject fresh life into the state's moribund farm belt. The college was a boon to Marshall, a neighborly, elm-shaded town surrounded by cornfields, one of which became the site of the $40 million campus. Southwest's ambitious little theater now delivers culture to the countryside, and class buildings are linked by passageways designed to accommodate wheelchairs, a feature that attracts handicapped students."

I wasn't aware that Southwest was designed to accommodate wheelchairs. I have no remembrance of any particular thought about this; I was going there to teach and that was my focus. As a matter of fact, I had had little experience and very little exposure to individuals with disabilities. I can only recall four with whom I had any significant contact.

The first, whom I never considered as handicapped, was my grandfather on my father's side. We called him "Paw Paw." The family story was that the eldest grandchild could not say 'grandpa' and it came out 'paw paw.' This name stuck with him.

He lost part of his right hand in a shotgun accident when he was a very young man, around twenty or so. Because of gangrene, he required a number of amputations, without anesthetics, eventually leaving him with a short stub below his right elbow. I can't even begin to believe what pain and agony this must have involved.

He had been right-handed. I remember that he was very proficient with his left hand, and recall watching him carpenter as he made small pieces of furniture for his granddaughters for Christmas and he continued to work in a sawmill.

I also remember that to shake his hand, he would reach out with his left and reverse his hand just as though he were shaking with his right. I never remember him talking about his arm or the lack of it. And God, was he strong in his left arm and hand! I once saw him take a big nail, drive it into a piece of lumber with his thumb and then he would drive the nail home with only two smacks of his hammer that would take a 'normal' person four or five strikes.

He was just "Paw Paw", my grandfather, nothing less, and nothing more.

There was a kid named Bobby. Bobby lived three houses down from us on Maple Street, in Roxana. My dad told me he had a condition known as cerebral palsy. I had no idea what that really meant. I only knew he couldn't walk, couldn't talk very well, had to stay home and couldn't go to school. Beyond that, I can't say I knew much more and didn't think about it too much.

I would see him sitting out in his backyard and every once in awhile he would be pushed over to the school playground. My dad and mom told me what they knew, so I wasn't afraid of him. I can say I never considered him a 'freak' or anything like that, but I was not too comfortable around him. He would have violent seizures. We kids called them 'fits.' These happened frequently as I recall, several times a day. I learned to leave him alone during these times, or make sure he did not hurt himself. His dad or mom seemed to materialize quickly and take charge. I'm sure they were watching him.

He stayed home when his parents refused to institutionalize him. I always thought that had to be hard. I knew he needed round the clock help with feeding and having all his other needs met.

Sorry to say, we kids in the neighborhood would tell each other that we would go get Bobby when one of us could not do something right, thus being a 'klutz.' How cruel of us.

I think his parents are dead and he is in an institution. He must be sixty or so, not too bad for a person who wasn't supposed to live beyond childhood.

Then there was Harold Dean. He drove my mother nuts. He was a paperboy and would have to be up around six or so to get his papers folded and delivered before seven. I would help him every once in awhile. Anyway, he would be down at my house by eight to wake me. I hated to get up. My bedroom window was in the back of the house. Mom and dad's bedroom was next to mine. Harold would call my name to wake me up, and when this didn't work he would throw small sand pebbles against my window. This woke my mother, and I can still remember her on many occasion yelling to me to get up and tell Harold to be quiet! Trust me when I say my mother had a way with words. But we would be off for the day to deliver those papers or to play ball.

Harold was a year or two older than me. His family lived down the alley on another street. The whole family was nearly or completely deaf or as my Granddad would say, "Deef 'n dum." Dum' they weren't. Harold and his older sister were always "straight A" students.

Hearing problems did not stop Harold from playing ball or much else as I can remember. He wore a hearing aid attached to a cigarette sized battery pack, which he would carry in his shirt pocket. He had to deliver papers in the afternoon, so this was our break time. We would all go home and eat and meet back at the ball field around six. This worked out pretty good.

No one thought too much about his deafness. But every once in awhile when he was wearing his hearing aid we would suddenly pretend to be talking to each other. Harold would take out his battery pack and shake it thinking the batteries were going dead or there was some connection problem. He would lean in towards us while trying to 'fix' his aid.

We would wait until we knew he had turned up the volume and then shout at each other, which of course was amplified and would blast his ears. We would laugh and laugh. And run.

Funny thing, this would piss him off and he would throw the gizmo on the ground and chase us. I as one of the smallest, I was usually the one he caught. It took me awhile to figure out who the real joke was on. I went home with many a split lip or bloody nose before I caught on.

When I was a freshman in high school there was a girl in a wheelchair. She was a senior. Can't be sure of her name. I think it was Mary. All I can remember is the football guys would carry her up and down the stairs to her classes.

My best childhood friend, Delton Phelps had a younger brother, who was deaf and attended a state school for persons with hearing impairments. His brother would come home to visit for short periods of time, usually during the summer. He could lip read and Delton would sign with him and then inform the rest of us what his brother was trying communicate. His brother was always involved in all our activities when he was home, so I must admit I never considered him to be a person with a disability.

These few experiences were not much in the way of awareness or understanding disabilities and the life experiences of individuals with disabilities. I was just a small town kid with his own little world to worry about. And that was a full time job. It was now time for my education into this new world to begin, an education that has continued to be part of my life now for over thirty years.

2

No Clue

It was late in October during the '69 Fall Quarter of my first year at Southwest. I was very pleased with the way things had gone. My families move, via U-Haul had gone well without many problems. My family, wife and four-year old daughter were living in an apartment complex just down the road from the college and we all seemed to be adjusting rather well.

As I recall, the weather that fall was gorgeous with no hint of a brutal winter. The fall colors were absolutely beautiful. The students at Southwest were really neat kids and so far my teaching was a pure joy. Illinois seemed like a distant memory although I did miss some of my good friends. But we were making new friends and getting situated in a very new environment. I doubt if any of my family had time to think back or become bored.

College teaching was totally different from teaching in high school. When I had no classes, my time was my own. And I wasn't teaching six and seven hours a day plus have hall duty and lunch room duty. There are no discipline problems to speak of at the college level. If a student misbehaves, you can dismiss them, with few, if any questions. So, all in all, I thought that the move had been a very good decision to this point.

I was in between classes and was going to the Department Office to check on my mail or some such thing. Actually, I probably was looking for someone to go down to the Student Union for a cup of coffee.

Southwest was a maze of tunnels which connected the three academic buildings at this time, the central academic complex, a theatre complex, and the physical education complex. I remember this gave me a feeling like one of Skinner's rats. I got turned around rather frequently, or at least I had to think about where I was and where I wanted to go. I may be a slow learner, but with time, I'm trainable. Over the years as the school expanded with new buildings this orientation continued to be interesting.

But it was also a Godsend. In the winter going from one building to another did not include going outside. Three cheers for accessibility and to the people who were responsible for designing and building a barrier free university.

In addition to all my other adjustments, I could not but notice the number of students in wheelchairs. I can't say I was bothered or anything, but they did seem to be everywhere, including my classes. I don't recall thinking about or being stunned or bothered; just that there were a lot of them.

I was, as I said, in-between classes and had turned the last corner towards the Department Office when I saw two students in the doorway talking to Wally Sande, Chair of Health and my boss. As they were blocking the door I stopped a few feet from them. I heard Wally tell them that he just didn't have the time and that he was sorry. Then pointing to me he told them who I was and that maybe I would be interested. And with that quick introduction, he disappeared back into the office area leaving the three of us standing there looking at each other.

"Good move Wally, one damn quick and easy way out of a tough situation." A real neat retreat!

"In case you didn't catch my name, I'm John Schatzlein," one of the students said. John was in a wheelchair and he pushed toward me extending his hand up to me. He seemed to be in his late teens or early twenties, pretty hefty with a good, firm handshake as he pushed towards me.

I shook his hand and reintroduced myself and extended my hand to the other student who identified himself with a short, "Curt Kettner." He was rather tall and slim and seemed a bit older, with a well-trimmed beard. He was standing, using crutches that had a cuff affair that fit around his forearms.

I remember mumbling something to the effect, "What can I do for you?"

John responded, "We are looking for someone to help us start a wheelchair basketball team."

There was a pause. No one said anything for a few seconds. "We need a faculty person to sponsor or coach us," John continued. "Curt and I have played before and will help someone learn about the game, but we need to have someone to schedule gym time for practices and generally organize us."

We talked a bit. I told them I had coached in high school for some eight years, but had made a decision to get out of coaching and just teach. I think one could say I gave them the usual 'song and dance' about how tough coaching was on my family with all the hours and travel.

I don't think they were impressed.

After about five minutes or so I did give them the old, "Listen, I'll consider your offer and talk to my family and get back to you." Does this sound familiar? The old, I'll get back to you, dodge.

They shook their heads and both of them rolled their eyes with the o'yeh, we've heard this one several times today look. I remember this quite vividly. John did offer that there was going to be an organizational meeting Thursday evening and since this was Tuesday, could they have my answer the next day?

I said *yes* to this and entered the office area. As they turned to leave they were mumbling to each other. I have always wondered what they were saying, but have never had the guts to ask. Sometimes it is better to leave well enough alone. I was intrigued and interested.

That evening I did discuss the offer with my wife using all the skill I could muster to convince her it would be a good involvement. In retrospect, I think I had made up my mind and wanted to accept not too long after the doorway meeting. Coaching was something that I enjoyed. I love the excitement, the challenges, and all that good stuff. And maybe, I also like being in charge, the authority—Naw, not Lew Shaver.

There came that moment in my discussion with Carol, my wife, that really made me pause. Other people seem to know us pretty well, ever notice that? I think sometimes some of us fool ourselves into thinking otherwise. Anyway, Carol asked me about my motivation, my reason for wanting to coach these kids. "Was it so that others would look at Lew Shaver and think what a wonderful person he is for working with the handicapped or is this something I would really like and enjoy doing?" she offered.

One's ego is an interesting thing, right? I told her and myself that I was going to give up coaching when I considered shifting to college teaching. Have to admit, I may go to my grave still pondering this question. But at the time, it seemed like the thing to do.

The next day John and Curt found me in the Student Union, having coffee sometime in the mid-morning. I told them it was a go if they were still interested. They thanked me, let me know when and where the meeting was going to be and left. It was really that simple. I just happened to be in the right place at the right time as I reflect back.

Our First Meeting.

In those early days at Southwest, construction seemed to be something that was always present and forever. This was the third year, having opened in the fall of

'67 and due to federal and state start up support, there seemed like a bottomless pit of money for development of all types of programs. I had heard that this wasn't going to last but for another two or three years, but in the meantime it seemed as if anyone could dream it, it happened. These times don't happen very often in one's life and the time was now, think it, do it, develop it, make it happen! Don't worry about tradition, be creative, and let it all hang out. This was true not only in curriculum development but in services programs, athletics, innovative technology; name it and it was a candidate for development.

In this vein, the wheelchair sports program seemed like the thing to do. Not only was the college accessible attracting a significant number of students with disabilities who had been denied access to higher education, there was a feeling that the college experience ought to be more than just the academics.

I happened to be down in the Business Services for some reason, which I can't remember on Wednesday and saw Curt sitting at a desk and acting like he really belonged there. When he saw me he motioned me over. Asked what he was doing, he informed me that he was not just a student but a working-student, his major being in business. Furthermore his wife was the college librarian. I visited with him for several minutes in which time he expressed his views about why the school needed to develop programs and services for the disabled just as for anyone else. I left this conversation, in retrospect, thinking this was his way of letting me know what was the right approach or at least his perception of what should be done.

The meeting room was a temporary classroom located in the lower floor of the physical education building. The meeting was scheduled for seven. As I walked down the hall I was met by John and Curt and informed that John would introduce me and that it was my meeting afterwards.

There were eight to ten people already there and of course one came late after five minutes or so. John introduced me and moved away leaving me standing alone.

There were at least a half-dozen sitting in wheelchairs. They had moved the regular desk to make room for their chairs, but I noticed a couple of empty wheelchairs. These two had evidently transferred to a desk—why, I didn't know, but took little notice. I saw several pairs of crutches and noticed there were different kinds. But what I noticed more than anything else was the silence and their stares. It was show time!

I reintroduced myself, gave a bit of background information and then asked them to sign up on a legal pad that I would pass around. I asked them to indicate their class status, freshman, sophomore, etc., and age.

While this was being passed around, it occurred as it always does in a group like this. Upon receiving the pad one person asked if anyone had a pencil he could borrow; never fails, seems like there is always one or more that need a pencil. I remember thinking, "Nothing new." Someone made a wise crack about college students should always have a pencil to which the pencil-less one uttered something to the effect that they just wanted a damn pencil, not a sermon. Nothing new. I don't know what I had expected, but I suspect I had some uncomfortable thoughts with the group and how they would react to any of this.

I'm not one to demand that people 'share' much about themselves at meetings such as this, so when I got the legal pad back and to make sure everyone had signed it I went through it calling out their names and asking them to identify themselves. I got a few "here's", a couple of "yo's", and some undistinguishable grunts.

Of course Schatzlein and Kettner I already knew. Then I continued with Stuewe. Believe it or not I correctly pronounced his name. Yes, way to go Lew. There followed Neutgens, Tusa, Guetter, Jacobson, Hansen, Van Buskirk, Anderson, and O-my-God. I was stuck, big time, a Scandinavian, Norwegian, or whatever you find in Minnesota and I quickly gave up and spelled it so the person could tell me without all the embarrassing attempts on my part. I spelled BJERKSETT, and was informed it was pronounced Berkset with the 'E' sound somewhat funny—I didn't ask, just listened to his pronunciation.

I concluded the meeting with a bit of my coaching philosophy. If I was going to do this it would be 100%. I was intense. I was demanding and very verbal without demeaning anyone. In short there would be one coach—ME!!!!!!! I emphasized that I worked hard at not using the word stupid or like words, but when I said something I expected, no demanded, that it get done. And last I made them a promise I would treat them like athletes, that John and Curt had emphasized this to me.

I also told them I had little knowledge about the game itself and even less about disabilities and wheelchairs. They all seemed to grin and let me know they would 'help' me. I told them I would check with the powers to be such as the Athletic Director about budget and scheduling gym time for practice and 'all those good things' and get back to them within a week or so.

And lo' and behold, there were no questions. Meeting over.

There I was, organized and ready to go, not sure where I was or exactly for that matter where I was going. Not a good thing usually, but this seemed to be okay at the time. The next few days I met with the Athletic Director, Glenn Mattke, got his go ahead on a trial basis with the support, which would include allocating gym space for practice and some basic equipment, namely a few basketballs. Glenn did ask about what the wheelchairs would do to the gym floor. I was ready. John and Curt had informed me that the chairs would be padded and the tires would not harm the floor. I told Glenn this with a deep conviction of reality and prayed it was the God's honest truth.

After consulting with the Physical Therapist, I found out that the college had purchased ten, street model wheelchairs through a federal grant to be used for wheelchair sports. I was to find out these were not suited for basketball or any other sport for that matter, but at the time I didn't know the difference between a competition chair and a street model chair. Hell, I didn't know anything about the damn things. But my enthusiasm sure sustained me regardless of ignorance.

I was on my way; there were ten or eleven players and their rookie coach.

Shortly thereafter the college newspaper ran an article, which proclaimed, "Southwest students and local fans will see a new kind of basketball this winter—the exciting display of the college's wheelchair team." It went on to say, "The new concept is characterized by handicapped persons…some…haven't been able to walk for years." The article finished with, "Coach Shaver, who has never coached a team similar in his life…will tell you. It's an altogether different world when you get into the chair."

The truth was I really didn't have a clue, but I was about to find out.

The KISS Theory.

I was being my brilliant self, waxing eloquent as is said. And some of us, especially coaches, can wax more eloquent than others. My second and third practices had gone well. I was 'feeling my Cheerios', my confidence growing with each practice that I could do this. And so away I went with my explanation, after explanation, after…!

As a matter of fact, according to a few of my friends, well maybe many of my friends, I have a difficult time saying anything in less than thirty minutes.

But never mind, I'm sure that on this occasion I was being brilliant.

The topic of this practice, after warm-ups and some shooting drills, was to explain the pick 'n roll, ala wheelchair basketball.

No need to bore you with the nuances in detail. I was instructing the team in the critical importance of the technique and of courses my mastery of it.

With each explanation of the various types of picks and the resultant outcomes came a floor demonstration with precise, detailed teaching of the wheelchair positioning and pushing mechanics. I was using a sort of show and tell approach.

Damn, I was on a roll and was magnificent. At least in my own mind I was.

But as I was about to learn, I was disregarding two, rather basic principles of learning.

The first and very basic one was to Keep It Simple Stupid (KISS). Later on in my teaching and coaching I would modify this to Keep It Short and Simple, as I realized that the word Stupid implied too much of a negative connotation, both for the players and myself. My explanation at this practice was being neither short nor simple.

The second principle ought to have been even more obvious, even to me. That is, the mind can only absorb what the rear end can endure. The wheelchair obviously magnifies this process. This had been some fifty minutes of rather dull and boring material and even worse, not much activity. There was lots of sitting and listening. Well, lots of sitting anyway. Can't vouch for the listening. No 'learn by doing' in this practice.

I was about to be reminded.

I completed my intense instruction, paused and in my best instructors' voice asked, "Any questions?"

Now I really know better. Only time there are questions are when the students or players want to kill some time so they don't have to learn anything else for the day. I just loved a teacher that we students could get going on something completely off the subject until the bell would ring. Chalk one up for the Good guys. Once again, there are those of us that will ramble on and on.

On the other hand, if the time of the practice or session is almost over before this question is posed, not many are silly enough to ask a question, which would prolong the agony. No sir, and any one goofy enough who does ask gets some pretty hard looks from the rest of the class, I mean being an 'apple polisher' or a 'teachers pet'. How about just a plain old 'ass kisser'.

Certain that I had covered all the material, dotted all the "i's" and crossed all the "t's" I was ready to announce that after a two-minute, all out push up and down the full length of the floor, practice was over. I did not notice a player pushing up behind me. He tapped me on the hip and as I turned around, he asked, "Lew, uh, what's a pick?"

"Holly shit," I thought. Isn't this something? Somewhere that little bit of information got lost, or wasn't there in the first place.

So I asked, "Anyone else that doesn't know what a pick is?"

Hell, nearly every hand went up. They had set while I talked and had no clue. And evidently, too afraid to interrupt and ask. Might make them look stupid. Right?

I excused practice asking the young man who had first let me know I had failed to determine what they knew in the first place to stay and talk to me for a few moments.

He then, quietly and very patiently, told me that for many of the players all this sports stuff was new. As a disabled kid, many of the players were not allowed to play on the playground or to have gym or physical education. He, for instance, was sent to study hall and generally excluded from what he described as any real life activities, especially those that were particularly physical in nature.

"I sure sat a lot and observed a lot, but always on the edge of the playgrounds, or on the blacktops and sidewalks. I was treated like a little china doll, I would break or something," he said.

I thanked him for his honesty and his patience and told him I would work hard not to take any of this for granted, but to remind me when and if I did.

He just smiled and let me know it would be a pleasure.

What's In A Name?

We had been practicing for a week or two after we had organized into what we thought a team should be when one of the players rather casually mentioned that perhaps we ought to think about what we were going to call ourselves.

Being a new school, Southwest was unique in that it had no tradition. We were building the tradition. This was pretty heady stuff. This was a new school, new curriculum and program development—fun stuff.

Our athletic teams, men and women, shared a common theme, a horse, with different names. The men were known as the Golden Mustangs and the women were the Pintos. I always thought this was a neat idea. If I read the local newspaper or any media account of Southwest athletics, I would immediately know what team had played without any reference to gender such as the "Lady Mustangs". I was always struck by and thought it was rather ridicules to read about sports teams and have them referred to as "Lady" anything. Sorry, but to be labeled as a "Lady Bulldog" or a "Lady Anteater" for example wouldn't be my idea of an appropriate state of affairs. I suppose those in Georgia and California might disagree, but that's the way I feel; I mean, ugh, Lady Bulldogs, Horn Frogs, etc.

And here in River City, at little old' Southwest, viola, the problem was solved. A real none issue. I thought it was brilliant. But sometimes I'm easily impressed.

So, what the hell, we decided to have a meeting and discuss the options. I scheduled a meeting, actually I think someone else did, but this is my story. We met down in John Schatzlein's apartment around seven. This was part of some of the new and innovative creations at Southwest. A series of four mobile home-like structures in a quadrangle, grouping pattern without any real control by the school. This was a pure free-market venture. These set off the campus and all were advertised to be accessible. The students labeled the resultant dwellings "sin city". Some of us were just born too early.

Any way several players showed up along with friends and camp followers. Hey, we were inclusive, a real cross-cultural effort before we even knew such a thing existed. Yes-sir, no discrimination here.

Of course John led the discussion. A bit awkward and clumsy for me, but being a democratic endeavor, and me being not one to try to dominate the proceedings, the discourse went on for some time with very little progress. That I could see, anyway.

God, everyone had input. And of course two or three at a time. This seemed to go on forever but was only thirty minutes or so. Finally, someone, don't remember who, it was just a voice to me, yelled loud enough to drown out the others that to differentiate wheelchair basketball from the other teams, the media would probably refer to us as the "Rolling Mustangs" or the "Pushing Pintos". The consensus was quick and rather unanimous we wanted to part of this.

Besides, it was getting late and I think the beer supply was running low.

From this statement, the discussion turned to labeling and how many of the people in wheelchairs felt labeled enough, as cripples and of course victims among the more mild references.

I sat and listened. Honest. Even I was surprised. I sat and listened. I seemed to realize this was great shit and I had no clue.

And then came the zinger. Someone expressed that under no circumstance would they want to be labeled onto something akin to the "Special Olympics", adding, "We aren't against the Special O, but we get confessed enough with being something other than normal to have a 'special' name-tag."

Whoa, this really woke people up. Some even stopped drinking. You know this must be a hot item. The talk became animated. No, it became boisterous as well as loud and not the least bit angry. The pros and cons of the Special O were flying back and forth. The main criticism, as I could make out from the scraps of verbalization I could hear and semi understand, was that given the legitimate intention of Special O, the problem lay in the marketing. I heard one voice proclaim, "Hell any one with a handicap is also treated as mentally retarded."

I think I was getting a headache. But I hung in there.

All of a sudden out of all the babble came a loud and I mean loud voice, "I got it dammit, I got it, what about Broncos? This keeps the horse theme, but makes us unique".

I kid you not, there was silence, refreshing and welcomed quiet.

Schatzlein seized the moment after a few seconds and simply said, "Shall we vote? All in favor of the Broncos say 'Aye'".

I was not sure that Roberts Rules would have sanctioned the proceeding, but it seemed as though it was unanimous.

And then a very positive voice rang out, "Let's go celebrate". Everyone knew what that meant, to the local watering hole. I was amazed at how quickly the place cleared out. I didn't know three wheelchairs could fit through a doorway, but sure looked that way, as within moments John and I were the only ones left and we were not going to be far behind.

As I left, I just gave John a 'thumbs up' and thought to myself, "We done good" as my old Uncle Pete used to say.

In the nest few days I submitted the name and rationale to Glenn Mattke, the Athletic Director who approved it and forwarded it up the chain of command until it received university approval. It was really that simple. The faculty assembly then voted to accept the name to make it official. I was amazed as even the smallest change in the structure of a university can take years. I've seen the faculty assembly for instance argue about one word, one damn word for forty-five minutes and still not come to a resolution. But this happened in less than two weeks if memory serves me well.

It was a decision we were to live with for some twenty-five years. There was a satisfaction in knowing that when people heard or read about the Broncos, They would know it referred to our wheelchair athletic teams.

At the time, I thought it was an important decision and quite honestly still take some pride and satisfaction.

A Lesson in History.

It wasn't until our second year (1970–71) that I really became acquainted with the history and foundations of the sport. We had been around the block for a year and had learned the basic requirements of what we needed to do to compete in the sport. We had become a member of the National Wheelchair Basketball Association.

In addition to the general requirements for university enrollment such as academic and housing issues, the wheelchair basketball 'wanabe' needed to be classified in wheelchair basketball, another label, another 'pigeon hole', as one student put it with some rancor. Another evaluation, another categorization process as some others expressed. I think I detected some negative vibes.

Right-wrong, good-bad, yes-no, who knows. But it was reality if a player wanted to participate.

I had received the rules and regulations from the national wheelchair basketball association office. This was located at the University of Illinois. I also received some information on the history of the sport I learned from this material that the game began after World War II with the return of a lot of guys who were paralyzed as the result of the war. One interesting item was the reference of these veterans being 'confined' to a wheelchair. I shared this with a few of our players and got an immediate response about the absurdity of this statement. As one said, "Hell, it sounds like we eat, sleep, go to the bathroom in this damn thing." I think I remember responding with a brilliant, "oh."

Out of this beginning, I learned that these veteran's, as young, red blooded American boys with lots of energy, goals, dreams, and drives not all of which are associated with sex found an outlet—good old competition. The reference to drives and sex is purely mine, my interpretation.

"And as God said, let there be wheelchair basketball. And there was, and it was good." So good in fact, that soon a national organization was established to govern the play, the National Wheelchair Basketball Association (NWBA).

The rulebook indicated that the game is played in accordance with NCAA rules with a few exceptions. These deal with the impact of the wheelchair that it has on the game. For instance, the wheelchair is defined in terms of dimensions, with characteristics legislated as to size, etc. The contact that is inherent in any basketball game is defined within the rule that the chair is part of the person. Other than these, with some minor variations, it is a basketball game. There are jump balls, fouls, traveling—a basketball game.

The rule for eligibility to participation states that anyone with permanent, lower limb disability or comparable disability is allowed to participate, not just those with spinal cord injuries. My suspicion, since I wasn't there in those early days and years, is that it soon became apparent that a 'cripple' wasn't always a' cripple' by any other name. There were differences, big differences. A person with a minimal disability, such as a foot amputation fit the permanent disability definition and would tend to dominate someone with spinal cord injury who could not twist and turn, nor lean and reach without some difficulty. I think I could imagine the scramble to recruit players with these 'minimal disabilities' whatever that may have been. This was all in the name of competition. Ain't winning interesting. Sure is.

Thus the classification system seemed to be developed to ensure and encourage the more 'severely' disabled to participate. With some variations and adjustments, the system has reflected three different levels of disability. Each of three classifications are given a numerical value with a maximum point total that may be on the floor at any one time, with Class I being the most severely disabled followed by Class II and the least severely disabled Class III.

At no time in a game shall a team have players participating with total points greater than twelve. There is an additional restriction in that there may be no more than three Class III's in the game at any one time. This adds an element to the game that is unique to the sport. It is a technical to violate the point total rule. As I learned, this does make substituting interesting from time to time.

To administer this process, the NWBA certified individuals to be classifiers, which included medical and physical therapist. I was very fortunate to have a physical therapist, Dan Snobl who became certified. Therefore, every fall, Dan would evaluate our new players for classification. There were forms to be completed and then submitted to the national office.

As an institution, Southwest attracted the student who tended to have a more severe disability because of our accessibility. This had the effect of fewer 'minimal' disabilities attending, as they did not have the problem of accessibility. Class III's sometimes were scarce and at a premium. There were years, as I was to experience when we would have only one or two Class III's. This does not mean we could not or were not competitive, but compared to national powers across the country, most of the teams had three Class III's and perhaps one or two more on the bench. This would be in addition to good Class II's and Class I's. Most often I would see three Class III's, a Class II, and a Class I on our opponent's starting team.

I'm not complaining—whining maybe, but not complaining.

I came to learn that not all disabled individuals are 'poster children' and want to play, even though Lew Shaver is the coach. Hmmm, maybe it was because yours truly WAS the coach. Nah!!

And would I lobby the Physical Therapist and lend my expertise in the classification of a player. To be honest, if there were a chance for a player to be classified as a II and not a III, thus enhancing the team. Let's just say I would drop a hint or at least give my distinguished opinion. Money was too obvious!! And Dan was a hell of a lot bigger than me, plus he was a professional.

And would a coach suggest the player fake, cheat, or at least feign cooperation with the Doctor or the Therapist? God forbid.

Think these things (shenanigans) haven't and don't go on? Heavens, not disabled people acting so normal.

In addition to the classification process material I received from the NWBA was an article that dealt with the history of the sport.

The following is an adaptation of that article written by the late Harry A. Schweikert, Jr., which appeared originally in the May 1954 issue of *PARAPLEGIA NEWS*. It has appeared in updated form in almost all National Wheelchair Basketball Tournament (NWBT) programs from 1954 to the present and represents the unofficial history of the game. He wrote:

There were a lot of guys who returned from the Second World War pretty well paralyzed and confined to wheelchairs for the rest of their lives. They were in the same bracket, had the same problems and frustrations, and the same unbridled and unchanneled energy. They had to find an outlet somewhere. Where better than in the red-blooded province of sports?

It started with such sports as ping-pong, playing catch, pool, then from bowling, swimming and volleyball to the more energetic water polo, softball, touch football and basketball. While many other sports have been added since that time, it was basketball that in a few years far out shadowed the others in popularity.

While the California Chapter of Paralyzed Veterans of America has been popularly credited with the birth of wheelchair basketball, the New England Chapter of the same organization offered documentary evidence antedating the California's claim to fame. Both will agree, however, that it started sometime in 1946 in the Veterans Administration Hospitals. Thereafter, it spread across the nation to VA hospitals in Boston, Chicago, Memphis, Richmond, and New York. Before long the sport had spread across the border to Canada and across the ocean to England.

By 1948 there were six teams in the United States, all members of the Paralyzed Veterans of America and all functioning from VA hospitals. This was the year the Birmingham, California team received a sponsored tour, by plane to play paraplegic teams across the country. An immediate result of this first tour of the Birmingham Flying Wheels was the formation, in Kansas City, of the first wheelchair basketball team outside of a VA hospital. This first "civilian" hometown team was named the Kansas City Wheelchair Bulldozers, later the Kansas City Pioneers.

The Flying Wheels of California won the first National PVA Championship. Their moniker became well known because the Wheels made 10 cross-country tours. These trips did much for the publicity and popularity of wheelchair basketball, and therefore, in many ways, for paraplegics and other severely disabled persons.

...It was not long, 1948 to be exact, before the Kansas City team was joined by another hometown team, the New Jersey Wheelers, and the first college team, the University of Illinois Gizz Kids.

In April of 1949, a group of students from the University of Illinois, working under the inspired and tireless efforts of Tim Nugent, Director of Rehabilitation, formed the first National Wheelchair Basketball Tournament. That was the beginning of the sport, as we know it today. The National Wheelchair Basketball Association...are...directly related to the original plan made by the organizing group of disabled students under Tim's guidance.

...Nowadays, wheelchair basketball is an international sport...the Gold Cup Championships, contested by the world's top men's and women's teams and held every four years, has gained ascendancy as the dominant international competition. outside of the Olympic-year competitions.

...A women's division was created...in 1990–91 within the structure of the NWBA as well as an intercollegiate division, and a junior division...

On the international front, the sport has organized as the International Wheelchair Basketball Federation (IWBF) in 1990...

I felt I had a better understanding of just what it was I was doing, however, as I now realize it was just the onset of my educational process into this new world, and the learning curve was really just beginning.

3

The Learning Curve

We Don't Need You To Take Care Of Us.

I was wired. I was organized. I had every minute planned with a period for warm-ups, drills for laps, passing, pushing, shooting for half court and full court work.

I vividly remember my first practice. God, I wanted it to go well, to impress the players that I knew what I was doing. All did go well until we began the full court stuff. All of a sudden, about half way through practice, two of my players, namely Schatzlein and Steuwe, were going down the floor, on opposite teams, axle to axle, elbowing each other. I watched amazed and expecting them to back off but I began to think their wheelchairs were going to meld together due the friction from the wheels and other metal parts. Hot metal begins to emit a burning smell and the smell was definitely there. This was demolition derby, not basketball.

I was shouting at them to back off each other, but having no luck. I decided to see how far they would go before someone was maimed.

Sure enough, almost in slow motion, John's chair began to tip on two wheels and began to lean or maybe, more accurate, list to one side. This continued for several feet until the point of no return was reached and over the chair went.

I was absolutely horrified. I thought, "My God, he's going to kill himself." Stuewe continued pushing down the floor laughing his ass off while John, who was left in the dust, or on the floor to be more exact, was uttering curses of all descriptions.

The other players began to circle John and rating the fall as you would a gymnast, yelling that the fall was only a 2.4 or a 2.8 because he did not point his toes or keep his legs together. They were having a ball. I was bewitched, bothered and bewildered. And a bit pissed!

All I could really think about was this poor guy was flopping around on the floor with his legs flailing around as he rolled over and over as his wheelchair cart wheeled over and over until it righted itself and crashed into the wall at the end of the basketball floor. I'll never know how it did this, but dammed if it didn't.

I continued to stand at mid-court not really knowing or understanding what I had just seen. I was stunned. Stunned to see such a episode but also stunned that the other players were 'making fun of him.' I thought, "Wow, what a bunch of cruel SOB's". In truth, I didn't know what to think.

My almost immediate reaction, as the dust settled, was to rush out on the floor to help or rescue him. I'm not sure which or even if I recall any thought in particular about it. Maybe it was just an instinctive coaching thing or maybe it was just a reaction on my part out of amazement and just a bit of pity or overreaction because he was handicapped. I can't say for sure. But out I went.

One thing I do remember and will never forget was his reaction as he rolled over on his back, propped himself up on his elbows and glared up at me and snarled, "What the hell are you doing?"

I informed him I was going to help him. He told me to go sit down; he would let me know when he needed my help.

I know I started to say something, but thought better of it and began to retreat slowly back to the sideline from where I came. All the while I'm watching the situation play itself out before me. I figured, being a rookie, that this was the most prudent action at the time.

Stuewe, who had dumped him retrieved his chair, pushed it back out, and held it in place as John transferred back up into it.

Practice then continued as if nothing had happened.

Later, in the locker room, I bumped into Kettner as he was leaving. "Just a thought," he said, "We don't need you to take care of us or speak for us. We need you to coach us."

I'm sure I replied with something that was very profound—like, "gotcha."

I had survived my first practice. And with only one fight. I found out this was something to be proud of. I had learned that some of the players do not like each other. Can you believe that? I had also observed that some of them think their chair is a tank whose mission it is to destroy all the others on the floor. Others don't have any idea what's going on, never played much of anything. But I had worked them hard of about an hour and half with some good sprints at the end for conditioning and not the least little bit, discipline.

John and Curt and a few others had also offered what they understood about the game as far as strategy and chair technique in what I thought was a very positive way. No one seemed to be making a move to grab any power. All in all I was patting myself on the back.

I had stepped out into the hallway just outside the gym. "Damn," I thought, "I'm beat." We had just finished a tough hour and a half practice and I don't know how the players were feeling but I had worked hard and was feeling the intensity. It was a good feeling, I had pushed the players hard and they had responded with what I thought was a good intense effort.

My little four-year-old daughter, Lynette, had come over with me. She often came over and was immediately adopted as the team mascot. I mean a little, cute four year-old. We were practicing from six in the evening until seven-thirty or so and I could have her back home by around eight. I thought it was a neat opportunity for her to be around the gang. She seemed to love it and so did the players.

I was looking for her and calling her name. Several times during practice she had gotten into an extra wheelchair and go wheeling around down the halls or go back down to my office where I would leave out paper and pencils for her to draw and doodle. She would present me with her art and of course it would be posted up somewhere in my office for all to see. To say I had quite a collection would be an understatement.

Suddenly out of the gym came John with Lynette on his lap, and as they disappeared around a corner I could hear Lynette saying, "Go faster John, go faster."

They returned in a couple of minutes. She wanted him to continue, probably forever, but he begged off telling her that her dad had worked them too hard and he was tired. I broke in with, "Maybe I didn't work you hard enough if you still had energy to push around the halls with Lynette." Lynette told me, "Don't pick on poor John." Wow did he have her trained, or was it the other way around?

You Might As Well See What It's Like.

"Get in,"

"Do what?" I replied

"Get in."

"Yeah, right!"

At a practice during our second week, I noticed a couple of players had pushed an extra chair into the gym. Not being too bright, I thought nothing about it. Until.

"Listen, if you're going to coach us you might as well learn what its like to be in a chair. So get in."

How could one refuse such an offer? I got in. Damn the world got tall in a hurry. I looked around and every one was watching with grins like a shit eaten' cat. So I began to push.

For the remainder of the practice I went up and down the floor, very, very slowly.

For the next few days, actually it was weeks to be truthful. I always like to think of myself as a quick learner. Try, try, and try, again. Hey, I got better.

It did seem as though I was always going in the wrong direction. And when I got turned around, everyone was still going in the wrong direction.

Along the way I experienced endless suffering. My fingers caught in the spokes splitting my fingernails. My thumb caught on parts of the chair I didn't know existed. I would just get healed and I would catch something again. My fingers got smashed, caught in between two chairs, sometimes intentionally I thought. Not these little darlings. They would never do something like that. Get the coach, especially when he is in such an alien world and doesn't know better.

I found out the hard way not to wear pants with pockets—catches the thumb right on cue.

I think I found every hidden part that could catch or slice a finger, thumb, or the whole damn hand, all the way up to the elbow it seemed.

I never, never knew how much skin I had on my hand. Skin is just supposed to cover the hand, but in this case skin is for ripping and tearing.

My God, the blisters! The tires are murder! I tried gloves. I had seen a few of the students in wheelchairs wearing gloves around campus. Monkey see, monkey do. This only added to my difficulties and problems as the gloves made catching and shooting the ball even more difficult. Given my skill level leaves something to be desired in the first place, this only made everything worse. Gloves were not the answer.

I soon realized that only time and effort would determine my mastery. People kept running by me in the meantime. But I got better.

Thank God we had an excellent athletic trainer at Southwest with a heart. I spent many a minute in the training room and used more tape in this early phase than any three or four players. The Trainer, R.A. Colvin, was a transplanted Oklahoman, and did not join us until my second year at Southwest. I mention him know as he was to become my right arm or at least an extension of some sort. He became an official and traveled literally the world with the team. By the way, R.A. had with a stutter problem. Everyone called him simply R.A. and he would clobber me if I mentioned his given name. The kids would imitate him trying to tell them something. This group didn't care who you were or what your status or what uniqueness or handicap anyone had, everyone was fair game.

But, what the hell, they would refer to themselves and each other as gimpy and cripples or crips or God only knows what else.

They Don't Always Need Me.

We had finished another practice. I was just leaving the gym to our locker room, which was just across the hallway.

As I left I looked back to sneak a peek at David Van Buskirk, one of the ball-players still trying to transfer from the gym floor to his wheelchair. Moments before practice was winding down he had fallen out of his chair while leaning forward to pick up a ball. He wasn't in any danger and as it was our final drill I chose to leave it up to him to transfer back up into his chair.

We completed a couple of minutes with some sprints up and down the floor and most of the players had left the gym.

One player had stayed to help. I stopped in the doorway to watch, David, still on the floor. He was having a hell of a time trying to transfer. He was grossly overweight. As a post-polio, he was a quadriplegic as a result. The net effect left him impaired significantly in the lower extremities to such an extent that once, when X-rayed for a possible fracture of the kneecap, there was little bone to be X-rayed. His bones did not grow and mature in the normal way. He hand arm and some hand function impairment in addition to the lower extremity pattern.

I caught the other player telling him that he needed to learn to pick up a ball without leaning forward in his chair. In the meantime, David was not having any success, but I'm sure all this friendly advice did not escape him and was welcome.

He continued to really struggle with the transfer.

He was a pretty bright young man. He and a buddy of his, a paraplegic, which David describe as his comrade in 'Gimpland' worked for a time for the Security Office for the university. They were infamous for not allowing professors, students, it didn't matter whom, to access offices, classrooms or any other area without the proper identification. They would radio each other with their handy-dandy CB's when confronted with a problem and discuss the procedure using the police form of communication to identify the situation. I thought they were a stitch, but as usual I found myself in a minority. Certain administrators and professors, as I later heard, from David and his buddy, of course, were not enthralled with their actions. They were pissed and relieved them from this responsibility. The administrators and professors I talked to described their actions in various terms, 'Gestapo' coming to mind. Ah, power is grand.

David continued to struggle. The floor transfer is a bitch to begin with and David's arm impairment plus his weight wasn't helping the cause.

I listened as the two continued to talk about his predicament for a few moments making sure there were no injuries and walked slowly back out on the court where they were.

"You OK?" I asked.

"Yeah, I'm alright," he replied. "This transfer is tough. Anything below my chair is really tough for me, and it seems like everything is up to me!"

He was sweating like the proverbial pig. To say he was laboring would be an understatement.

We spent a few moments talking about the transfer technique. David discussed and I added what ever I could, which was limited. But I began to sound and act smart. The one thing we agreed on was that he certainly needed to get down to the therapy area and put in a lot of work.

The other player, who had hung around, offered a bit of wisdom. Sometime in the future, no one would be around to help him transfer and it might be a life and death situation and pretty scary stuff to think about.

I'm sure David loved all the advice and encouragement about life and death. Real comforting.

He lay there, sweating and swearing under his breath, but acknowledged our words, but I sensed he wasn't buying in to all this, especially from me, who was going to simply walk away, after all was said and done.

We agreed to allow him to continue trying to transfer while I went to the locker room to go to the bathroom and come back in a bit. I also had to put up the basketballs and equipment. I asked if he was going to be OK with this, as if he really had any choice.

Seeing I was not going to lift him back up by myself, he nodded his agreement. Or maybe he wanted to get rid of me.

It wasn't that I had all the knowledge or that I was all that bright, but I could see lifting someone of his dimensions might end up with my herniating or getting much shorter in stature. I was going to need help, as in a lift crane or some-such device. Not being cruel, just real.

Our gym is a recessed facility and people are always on the upper level above the floor observing whatever is going on below. Several students were watching this scenario. I thought little about this, probably not even noticing them.

In about five minutes I returned from putting away the equipment and going to the bathroom. As I reentered the gym I saw David still working hard. I had flagged down my student manager to come back with me.

David had scooted and pulled his wheelchair over to the bleachers and had worked out a position where he was trying to transfer up to the first level of the bleachers and then to transfer to his chair.

I walked over to him and for a few more moments we talked about his learning how to complete the task. I was impressed with his understanding of his predicament and his acceptance. As I said, he was a bright kid.

He was pretty well shot. Shit, he was exhausted. With the help of my student manager we assisted him back into his chair. He promised to check with the therapist about the technique and a program to help him. He was still squaring himself away as I left him.

As I stepped out into the hallway, I was greeted by an irate group of students. They had been watching our efforts from above. There were four or five of them, never could get a count as they were moving about while all the time working me over pretty good verbally with words like 'beast' and 'SOB' among the milder ones.

I was trying to explain, but they continued to let me know they had never seen anything so despicable. Their wrath was intense and without stoppage.

They were still working me over when David rolled out the gym door and found himself in the middle of this fracas.

He sat and listened for a few seconds and then in a very commanding voice interrupted the conversation. The polio had not damaged his vocal cords.

"Wait a minute," he shouted and then paused as the group quieted down. He looked up at them and grumbled as he pushed through, "He's right, get off his ass."

With that proclamation, he pushed through to the locker room.

I could have kissed him! The students were absolutely stunned and thankfully, silent. I shrugged and with a certain amount of satisfaction and glee, said under my breath, "I told you so."

I didn't wait for any response. Prudence is the better part of valor. I retreated while the getting was good.

A Mile Might Not Be Enough.

The whole table was in hysterical laughter.

The waitress was running back into the kitchen after throwing her order pad and pencil up in the air in total shock, terrorism, bewilderment, and God only knows what other reaction.

I sat amid this chaos thinking I'm surrounded by a bunch of crazes. I also wondered what the hell I had gotten myself into.

Here we were on our first road trip ever to anywhere. We were on our way to the Twin Cities area and had stopped around three in the afternoon at a roadside restaurant to eat a pregame meal. We were scheduled to play at seven-thirty that evening.

We had pulled into the parking lot of the restaurant. The two station wagons we were driving did not have hand controls, so by necessity, the drivers had to be able to drive without any modification. This was one of the primary criteria in selecting a student manager. The manager became a wheelchair repairman, score-keeper and all around pack animal for loading and unloading equipment, wheel-chairs and in some instances the players themselves. To say the least, I became protective and very friendly with my student-manager. This was an exulted posi-tion and these students were paid handsomely—just kiddin' as most were volun-teers or working with me for credit on an independent study basis. Cheap labor.

As we unloaded before going in to eat, I did notice some of the patrons in the restaurant were ignoring us, acting as though we were not outside. I thought this was somewhat odd. I know, in my life, I had never seen such a sight where there were a dozen or so handicapped individuals all in one place and under no appar-ent supervision. There were handicapped people all over the parking lot. There were amputees, post-polio's with sticks and crutches, paraplegics and quadriple-gics in wheelchairs and who knows what else. This was a real what's-what of the handicapped population.

The people in the restaurant that we could see through the big windows con-tinued to act as though we did not exist. I could see several at least glance in our direction and then quickly look away. I thought about what these people thought was going on. Don't stare at the cripples. The restaurant was about to be invaded by this invisible spectacle.

Maybe they thought that if they ignored this bunch, we would go away and they would not have to deal with the situation. I had never experienced anything quite like it.

As we began to filter in one or two at a time, the manager somehow identified me as the leader and obviously as normal. This was scary by itself. I still did not comprehend or have a clue what was going on.

The manager identified himself and asked me where they wanted to sit. A light bulb began to go, but still dim. I replied that they, and I emphasized they, were all college students, part of a wheelchair basketball team and independent. They could sit anywhere.

Then, in an obvious solicitous and exaggerated way the manager began to move tables and chairs all over the place until I stopped him and indicated the players could take care of this.

As we moved chairs out of the way I noticed the small children were staring. Their parents raised their eyes and just as quickly lowered them again. I heard one mother tell her two children not to stare at 'people like this'; it was not polite. I began to feel uncomfortable. Its like I was running a freak show or something.

One of our players, a double amputee, wheeled over to a table with a couple and a little girl and said something to the girl that I could not hear. Then I heard him respond to the little girls' question about what happened to his legs, that he had lost them in Viet Nam. Her little eyes got real big. Her dad told her to turn around and eat and not to bother the player.

I shook my head. The amputee had never been in Viet Nam.

After we were all seated and squared away the waitress came out. She came directly to me. The manager must have pointed me out.

She leaned over towards me and in the best baby talk asked, "And what would they like to eat?"

I really don't remember my initial reaction. I think it was rather one of being stunned. I sat there and looked up at her and shook my head. The light bulb was getting brighter.

Someone at the table offered a bit of advice in a very sarcastic tone, "Well coach, tell her what they would like!"

Finally I looked at her and said something to the effect that she should ask them what they wanted. I don't think this was what she wanted to hear. Her pained expression said it all. It was like—you mean I'm going to have to talk to them?"

She seemed to gather her wits, turned to the player next to me, good old John Schatzlein, and repeated her question, again in baby talk.

I was now in tune with the situation. The players were being treated as though they were mentally retarded. Come to think of it maybe it was more than just the players. Evidently she thought that if a person is in a wheelchair, there must be also be a level of mental retardation involved. This being my first experience with such a reaction, left me dumbfounded and without a clue how to respond. So I sat and let the scene play out. Sort of prudence being the better part of valor, or perhaps just my own ignorance.

As the waitress waited for some reply she leaned over toward John to write his order and to probably make sure she heard everything correctly. John began to talk. His words were slurred. He also began to move his head in uncontrolled motions, rolling it from side to side. He continued to slur his words and added body convulsions to his little act.

I was stunned and thought this was maybe not an appropriate thing to do. I also was thinking about what the hell had I got myself into. But at the moment I was a captive of the situation.

John continued this little charade for perhaps some ten to twenty seconds. God, it seemed longer. In the meantime the others players began to snicker, laugh, and what have you. They were obviously enjoying all this.

The waitress got this God-awful look of total disbelief. I'm not really sure I understood anything about what was going on or her reaction. What I did understand was what she did next. The pad and pencil had flipped straight up in the air and she ran, making sounds that I cannot describe, back into the kitchen.

And my little darlings—they were laughing their butts off as I sat without a clue, still wondering what the hell I had gotten myself into.

It took several minutes to explain to the manager what was going on. Its tough to explain something you don't have a clue about. I must have done some of it right as he began to settle down. He seemed pissed.

And all this time I continued to question what the hell I had gotten myself into. Am I repeating myself?

That's how I felt.

We did order, without further incidence. The original waitress did return with a couple of others. There is safety in numbers-right?

As the meals were served, the players shared with me some of their feelings when something like this happens, and they assured me it happens rather frequently.

I did suggest that the response might not have been appropriate, that it seemed they were making fun of people who were palsied. Some people, I suggested, may be horrified. I noticed I was doing a lot of suggesting. Not knowing what the hell was going on, it seemed like the only thing I could do. My little bit of philosophy was acknowledged, but also I was reminded that I had never been in their place before.

The conversation drifted into a more general focus on how many minorities are labeled and that discrimination does occur. I shook my head as though I understood, but I'm sure I really, really didn't.

As one player eventually said to me, "Until we walk a mile in someone's shoes or moccasins, how can anyone understand?"

I was still pondering this when another voice popped up, "Hell coach, a mile may not be far enough, and in this situation it's 'push' a mile."

Where Sympathy Is In The Dictionary.

"What a bunch of crap. To hear the news stories, everyone who is paralyzed is paralyzed from the waist down. I mean look at this para-belly. Does it look like I'm paralyzed from the waist down?"

I had never really considered this issue or for that matter even thought about it and not knowing what a para-belly was, was not about to ask. But then, I'm not in a wheelchair.

I was working on our competition wheelchairs in a small repair room of our main Physical Therapy area. This was a frequent thing. This seemed to be every night. Nights were made for wheelchair repair, right? Does this sound like whining or 'poor old me,' feel sorry for Lew talk? Perish the thought. The chairs during this time period, late 60's, early 1970's, were not built to take the abuse we gave them everyday, day in and day out.

The chairs were little regular street models. We tried to modify them as best we knew how. We were always trying to reduce the bulk and weight, as they weighed some sixty pounds. We would remove the brakes, the arm rests and anything else not welded down. We would cut and lower the back height for the players who did not need this type of support. Some players need almost none.

In our primitive way we were attempting to make the chairs more efficient and effective, 'user friendly.' Again, this took many an evening.

In the course of a day or evening effort, several players would stop by to give me any assistance they could. I always suspected they knew my mechanical ability rivaled my skill in brain surgery. Any help was welcome.

Once, when I was drilling a hole in a piece of metal, can't remember for what purpose, I was not doing very well. The drill and I were having a hell of a time making a hole. And the piece of metal was winning. I felt someone behind me and turned to see our Physical Therapist watching me and shaking his head. I never knew how long he had been standing and watching. He continued to shake his head as I continued to be agitated and cursing the metal, the drill, or any thing else I could blame.

After a few moments he grinned and said, "It works better in forward, not reverse," and turned and walked out of the room chuckling. I knew I had been had. Another Shaver story was born.

How was I to know the damn thing had a reverse? What does a drill need a reverse for anyway? I know, I know. To back out of a hole that was just drilled. Or hung up or…big deal!

I'm not too mechanically inclined. Some have suggested I'm a real klutz. But I try hard.

Good ol' John had pushed in and was sharing the newspaper article that indicated the 'waist down' crap as he put it.

"Isn't ignorance beautiful?" He continued, "And we are always referred to as them, or they, as if we are all the same."

I nodded in agreement.

"Another thing that frosts my butt is in every story about a disabled person, it always refers to our courage. God, I hate that word. There is nothing courageous about being in this damn chair."

I grunted and nodded. He was on a roll. "According to these stories, we are all victims and I love this, confined to a wheelchair, as if we never get out."

"You seem pissed," I said, somewhat pretending to be surprise at the outburst.

Wow, was he ever on a roll or a mission.

"If people really want to know what it's like to be in a wheelchair, we should give them a spinal block, dump'em out in some downtown area and let them find the accessible rest rooms," he almost snarled, not answering my comment about being pissed.

Again I nodded. "Hand me the duct tape, please," I said. I needed the tape to build up a footrest with some styrofoam on a particular wheelchair so one of our players could put his feet on the footrests. Some of the players have very short legs and they will just dangle if the footrests are not built up. I was learning that duct tape is the greatest invention since peanut butter. It will fix anything on a wheelchair it seems. It always reminded me of a farmers' use of spit and bailing wire.

"Anything else I should hear," I asked, trying to be funny.

John was in no mood for funny.

"And all those damn posters. Did you see the one that identified our team as 'the crippled students?' And of course the ones which always have a really cute little kid in braces and on crutches. God, what pitiful and pathetic BS. As if all of us need pity and of course we are all victims."

I handed him a screwdriver and ask him to work on a seat rail.

He worked for a few minutes. Actually he attacked the seat. He stopped working, sat back, put down the screwdriver and asked, "Does any of this make any sense?"

"I guess so," I said. "But I'm not in a chair, so it's hard for me to relate. It must be something like teaching. I mean, students sleep with their eyes open during my lectures and hell, they even smile at me. But how do I explain that to you? I don't know if this would have any meaning to you or not."

Obviously this did not impress him. I even wondered if it had any relevancy, but it seemed like I should say something.

"No, I mean it," he said, "I get tired of all this sympathy laden crap. Dammit, I'm independent and don't need any starry eyed 'do-gooder' to use me to raise money or to make themselves feel good by making me an object to be pitied."

He paused. To get a second wind I think.

I was not totally stunned. I had heard some of this before and had seen some of the reactions. I was beginning to understand some of the frustrations and of the pride and hurt when being treated differently.

"Hell, Lew, you can hate yourself and everybody who had something to do with my accident and live a miserable life. Or you can acknowledge the fact that you are not going to walk again, enjoy life and get the most out of it. I chose that route and I'm not one bit sorry," He shared with me.

"But it's difficult for me or anyone not in a chair to totally understand this," I said. "Hell John, I don't know what its like to be a female, a Catholic, Jewish or Muslim, or black or oriental, or, or, or. I can't know of all these things. I sure wish I could. Guess if I did I would write a book."

With that John sorta shifted gears and asked, "So what do you think about all this politically correct stuff? Shit Lew, what the hell is physically challenged? I mean, come on. I guess if one is fat, then they are horizontally challenged or if a person is short, they are vertically challenged, right? And if you are bald, you are follically challenged. Shit, this could be fun."

Once again he paused, glanced up at me and grinned. He took a breath and paused, but only for a moment.

"Just feeling some anger," he continued. "I tried to pull into the handicap parking space and some damn AB had their car parked in it. It just hit me wrong. I mean I'll trade my parking sticker for the use of their legs."

"Stereotype, stereotype, that's all some of this does. Does the ends justify the means?" He seemed to be asking me. But he did not wait for any response. "And all those damn thumbtacks that fall off bulletin boards and find their way into my tires."

He lost me on these last two statements. But I don't think he really cared.

"Don't have the answer to that John. It's getting late, let's get out of here and go home," was about all I could contribute.

"Thanks for listening," he said as he pivoted to leave. "All this reminds me of my Orthopod back in the hospital. He let me know what reality was and what sympathy for the disabled was going to be. He told me that sympathy could be found in the dictionary somewhere between the words shit and syphilis. I've never forgot that little slice of life."

I smiled and shook my head in an understanding way and promised myself I would remember where sympathy was in a dictionary. Neat piece of information.

Well, I'm not sure I got a lot of work done that night, but I think I heard some very significant feelings.

"Thank you," I said as I turned out the light and shut the door.

Just Who Is Handicapped?

"Now what," I mumbled.

The station wagon was slowly losing power and speed. I slammed the accelerator to the floor and pumped hard. No matter, the speedometer went down and down—55, 45, 35,…, 15.

The team and I were on our way to Grand Forks, North Dakota for weekend games. It was Saturday morning. We were scheduled to play that evening around eight o'clock and then again on Sunday morning at ten before returning home Sunday afternoon. It was a good six to seven hour trip, one way.

This had been an uneventful, typical trip with no problems up to now.

We were traveling in two station wagons with me in the lead and pulling our trailer with all our wheelchairs and gear. Yes sir, me in the lead going up Interstate 29. Not a care in the world. The usual conversations were going on, that is for those that were not asleep.

This is Red River Valley country, flat, mile after mile. The joke about this region, according to Minnesota folks is that it is so flat with so few trees that the state tree is the telephone pole. I'm sure North Dakota people have an answer for Minnesota. They point out that the state bird of Minnesota is the mosquito.

So much for folklore.

Nothing extraordinary had happened as we loaded earlier in the morning leaving Southwest around nine o'clock or so. This was late January. Of course it was cold. We were in Minnesota. The wind was blowing as it usually does on the prairie to go along with the minus-zero temperature to make the wind chill factor somewhere around a minus-fifty, give or take a few degrees. When it's this cold, it doesn't matter. IT IS COLD!!!!!!! It was always an adventure under these conditions to 'sally forth' as it were.

I had arrived at the school around seven after saying goodbye to my family. My kids would usually just grunt, roll over and pull the covers over their heads mumbling their profound love for me. After a quick breakfast and last kiss from the wife I was off to another adventure.

I had to drive out to the university maintenance area to the car pool to pick up the two wagons and the trailer. I always picked up the keys for the wagons on Friday before leaving school.

In addition to praying that my own personal car would start under these extreme conditions, there was always the worry about the two state vehicles starting. But, not to worry, almost every vehicle in Minnesota has an engine block heater. This is a device, as I understand them that keeps the water flowing through the engine block making it possible to start on cold mornings.

The heater is electric, so you plug it in at night. At home one would just use an outlet in the garage or one available from the house. Most apartment complexes and motels in Minnesota have outlets in their parking lots to service the dwellers. These lots take on a strange look what with all the extension cords which all seem to be a bright orange color running to each car. Orange shows up to better see in the snow, got that one figured out.

If it had not snowed the night before, you thanked God for small favors. We always carried a couple of extension cords on our trips to plug in the vehicles at our motel. When outlets were not available I would run the extension cords out a motel window. Don't ask, trust me, it works.

And, sometimes at work during the week, you had the pleasure of going outside in the parking lot to start your personal car every four hours or so. Sound like fun? You betcha!

If, by chance, it had snowed, I had the additional fun of cleaning off the snow and scrapping the ice from the windshield, doors and rear glass. Always a real fun job, but hey, what's fifty below if not to enjoy. Every so often, I would not have a real ice scrapper, and anything would do. The army called it field expediency as I recall. What ever works. Over the years I have used and watched others scrape using credit cards, belt buckles, finger nails, cassette tapes, cigarette lighters and last but not least or final, the good old crushed beer can. Again, whatever works.

It's a challenge, an adventure, right?

Some would and do characterize all this as a pain in the butt. But Minnesotans are tough, even those of us who were transplants. I'm not sure how bright we are, but boy are we tough.

On this morning all went reasonably well. By around seven-thirty I had started both state vehicles, plugged my own car in place of one of the state ones and had driven the short distance from the car pool area to the main academic complex. This was done by leaving one vehicle running at the motor pool, thus to be picked up at a later time when my help would arrive.

One of the, if not the, most important task after picking up the wagons was to make sure the players could get into the main academic buildings from their dorm area. Even though Southwest was accessible, the dorms were separate. They were close, but separate—no tunnels or such. This was a tough proposition on some early morning weekends.

A few yards of ice and snow can be an awesome push. Add the subzero temperature and there is the chance for an absolute disaster. My worst nightmare and fear was finding someone in a wheelchair frozen in front of a locked door.

Prudence is once again the better part of valor. To offset this situation, I had a set of keys and a plan. I checked out the building keys from out Student Affairs Office sometime on Friday and would make sure I told the team where and when I would open such and such a door on Saturday morning.

God help me if I forgot to do this. On second thought, God help the players.

If I did forget the keys, I went to Plan B, or my panic plan. This involved calling the University Security Office as soon as possible on Saturday morning after it dawned on me that I had forgotten. I would arrange to meet a security person down at my office and explain what I needed. This person invariably would inform me what I should have done which I already knew. Maybe I had interrupted their morning nap. I would listen, not well, but listen and then inform them that while we were discussing the issue and I was receiving my lecture on the proper protocol, some poor wheelchair person might be freezing. Nothing worked better. This usually brought about the proper response—go open the damn door.

I loved those lectures, they always made my day. Of course, if I did have the keys and forgot to turn them in on Monday morning, I would get lecture number two on how more responsible I should be. I'm not sure how many of these lectures I received over the years. I recall they were numerous. I thought this was a bit of double jeopardy.

The gang all showed up on time and at the right place this particular morning. As I hitched up the trailer, packed the gear, picked up the second wagon, helped transfer the players, folded and broke down the wheelchairs I often thought to myself, "I'll bet the coaches in the Big Ten and other NCAA Division I universities never enjoyed all these neat things. I mean, Bobby Knight probably never knew what he was missing. Just a thought.

On this morning all went well. On the road again.

Until.........The speedometer was down to 10 mph and still dropping despite my vocal encouragement and for all my foot pumping. Enough is enough. I signaled and pulled off the road to the shoulder. The wagon kept running, barely. I continued to mutter obscenities and smacking the steering wheel for good measure.

The other wagon had pulled off in behind me. I ran back to let them know something was wrong. Everyone understood that given what I knew about the internal combustion engine, which was as much as I knew about rocket science, we were in a bit of hurt.

I returned to my wagon. I had taken off my heavy coat after the vehicle had warmed up and of course did not put it back on when I ran back to the other wagon and was experiencing a near death experience by the time I climbed back in. I sat, shivering, and trying to think about what I could do—all the time getting all kinds of advice, which I acknowledged with my usual a kindness and thankful acceptance.

Then came the voice from the rear of the wagon, "Let me try to fix it." I looked in the rearview mirror and saw Mike roll down his window.

"What are you doing?" I demanded.

"I've got my tool kit with me and I think I can fix it, OK? Unless you would like to try?"

"Sure, OK," I said with resignation. I knew some of the players carried a small pouch with a few tools with them for wheelchair repair. I also knew this kid was a mechanical genius and given my total ignorance, it seemed like the thing to do.

But Mike was a high para and the thought did occur to me as to how he was going to manage the physical demands of the job. I was about to ask him if he needed his wheelchair when I saw him exit the rear window and disappear up on top of the wagon.

I could then hear him on top and then he was staring at me through the windshield—and making faces at those of us inside. Down the windshield, over the hood and with a cute little flip was bracing his self on the front of the wagon.

With an impish grin he asked me if I knew how to turn off the engine and release the hood. I think I called him a smart butt, but did what he asked. I also asked him if he needed any help.

"Are you kidding?" he answered, "You just stay warm and cozy."

See, he was a smart butt.

In a few minutes, after actually climbing into the engine area, he backed out and motioned for me to start the engine.

I did and it did!! It fired to full power.

Mike reached up and slammed the hood down, crawled back over the hood, waved as he went up the windshield, over the top and back into the rear window, to a rousing round of applause and congratulations.

I asked what he had done to which he replied that I really wouldn't understand, but did say something about a gasoline filter.

Smart butt!

We were back on our way and I would love to tell you all was well and good.

Not to be. This scenario was played out once more on our way up and once on our way home. Each time the same pattern:

Mike would roll down the rear window.

Mike would crawl out to the top of the wagon.

Mike would slide down the windshield, out over the hood.

Mike would crawl into the engine area, after which I would ably assist him.

And Mike would fix the damn thing and retrace his route.

And I would set, watching this paraplegic and wonder just who the hell was handicapped.

By the way, we won both games over the weekend.

You Can't Put People In A Box.

My God, they were all nodding their heads up and down with silly grins on their faces—all of them.

Only moments before I had introduced the guest to my class. I was teaching a course with issues of disability. Periodically, I would ask a student with a disability to share some of their life followed by a question and answer session. This was a particular unique experience for most people. Given the disabled student population at Southwest, I thought it was a natural extension to the class. I was careful to inform the guest that this was volunteerism and no restrictions would be placed upon them. It was their story and they were free to tell it in their own way.

This young man, sitting in his electric wheelchair, was trying to tell my class about his disability, cerebral palsy. He told, how, at birth, he had experienced a lack of oxygen that caused extensive brain trauma that left him with great difficulty controlling movement. He also had movements that would seem to come and go at their own pleasure. His speech was a series of mutated sounds, only understood by those really close to him. To quote him, "I was a mess."

He was trying to tell my class how; at about age four, he was judged to be severely mentally retarded and placed in an institution where he remained for some time until his parents, through tenacious efforts, convinced the powers to be that intellectually he was fine.

The problem was that his physical being was distorted. As a matter of fact it is my understanding his actual I.Q. was well over 120.

It took him several minutes of unintelligible speech to get this bit of information out. As he spoke, it became more and more evident to him that no one really understood him. But, they all were pretending to understand, smiling and nodding.

He paused and then began to call the students in the class names. Not polite mind you—names that questioned their mothers integrity and genealogy. These were the mild ones by comparison to the later names.

And my twenty or so class students? They continued to smile and nod.

The more names he called them, the more they smiled and nodded.

His head was bobbing and weaving like some prizefighter and he began to drool as he became more and more agitated.

He suddenly stopped and seemed to collapse due the exhaustion of his efforts.

And my class—yep, they continued to smile and nod.

I stopped the proceedings and asked my class to tell me what he had said.

No response. I mean absolute silence.

So, there we were, a room a full of silent beings with no idea what was happening or what to do.

Finally, one little voice in the back of the room broke the silence and asked, "We give, what did he say?"

After hearing reality, the discussion centered on why people react in such a way and what, as individuals we ought to consider. One student asked our guest if he would write to his feelings and would he come back later for another session.

He agreed and a few days later rolled into my office with the following. I thanked him very much and used his remarks for years as I taught about disabilities and adapted physical education. He titled his effort, *I Talk Too Slow, You Listen Too Fast:*

"I have a speech defect. People, especially total strangers, have a hard time understanding me. I sound sort of like a drunk except a lot worse. My tongue and lips and head move not enough and sometimes too much. This condition in caused by Cerebral Palsy, which means that my brain sends out the wrong impulses at the wrong time. As it is with so many handicaps, society's attitudes as a whole seem to be more of a handicap than the actual physical defect.

People react differently to me. Some are horrified. They run past me looking the other way. Sometimes in my braver moments I get a "Hi" before they are ten feet down the hall. Then there are those who don't talk to me, but to the person who's with me, "How old is he?" and "Does he watch TV a lot?" are some examples of this form of indirection. There are also people who say, "Hi, how are you?" and walk past me before I can give my most profound response to that most profound question, "OK." These persons use me as a pill for little ego trips. They are good and are seen by others as good if they speak to poor bastards like me. Then there are the pretenders. They nod their heads and move their hands in understanding gestures, but know no more than the man on Mars about what I am saying. They aren't pulling any wool over my eyes. I can see they are not with me on about the second word that comes out of my mouth. They're so afraid they might hurt my feelings if they ask me to repeat anything. It hurts me worse to see people so ignorant. I'm not a little baby that cries every time that I have to repeat something to somebody. Finally, there are people who truly try to understand me. It takes time and effort for them and for me. But after a while we can communicate about as easily as any two people. This last group makes all the rest bearable, and I don't think I could live without them.

Because of my speech, few people that don't know me will come up and start a conversation. This means if I want any friends, I have to put myself into situations where people are forced to talk to me that is until they can understand me. I have recently graduated from college and have adjusted well. Many times I have forced myself into professors' office to ask them questions that I already knew the answers to, just to get them used to me. Back in the dormitory, I go into people's rooms and ask them for things I don't need like glue of paper clips, then try and strike up a conversation with them. Girls, because they live in different dormitories, are harder to deal with. I usually ask them if I can use their notes or if they will type a paper for me. These methods work fairly well. I have gotten close to a few people, and I think they can adapt to the non-college situation as well.

Attitudes are a big factor in how people react to me and why I have to be so forceful if I want to get anywhere. People think an individual with a speech handicap is not quite a person. They don't understand why I can't talk right. Some think it's because I'm retarded. Some think I'm mentally ill. It's hard telling what people are thing. American society moves fast. People want to hurry up. They are too busy to talk and listen to normal speech. Even within the family, communication breaks down. What family ever sits down at meals any more? Everyone is in a hurry to go to bridge club or to a basketball game. There is a general tendency for people towards non-involvement. People are pushed into little boxes by themselves and by others. I don't feel human; I feel like a rat in a cage. In this kind of world, I can't really expect a stranger to talk to me, unless they are special.

I see many good things about having a speech handicap too. It helps me to know who the special people are. I know who is patient and considerate just because they reach out to me. Because I can't talk as much as others, I am a better listener. I'm not always worrying about what to say and can concentrate more on what people are talking about. And finally, I can talk behind people's back, so to speak. In high school, for example, my closest friends could understand me perfectly, but the teachers could not. I would swear at them and call them all kinds of dirty names, and my friends would laugh and laugh. The teacher would sit there dumbfounded, afraid to ask what was so funny.

It has been a real hassle even with my acceptance and adaptations. Even with my guts, I still fail. I can't count how many times I have chickened out, and how many girls have passed that I wanted to talk to. I wish more people had patience, had the time to sit down and talk to me. I wish society were not so greedy and so much in a hurry to go nowhere. But most of all, I wish I had more guts.

A Team Manager Is As Good As Gold.

"Hey coach, have I got a deal for you."

I was about to learn about another significant bit of handicapped life. I had no idea it was coming. I just loved learning something at the least expected time!

Our bus had stopped on one of our long trips to gas up.

This usually took about twenty minutes or so each time we would stop. An over-the-road bus could go many miles between fill-ups.

These stops were rather routine. Those that could walk, known as 'walkers'—clever, huh—would or could get off the bus for a potty break or to buy snacks or just to stretch.

There were always a few players who were semi-ambulatory—SA's for short—could, with assistive devices such as crutches, walk for some distance. They could or would also be able to get off.

Then there were the wheelchair or non-ambulatory players. They needed the wheelchair to traverse the universe. Unless someone could or would retrieve on of the wheelchairs packed in the bay of the bus or we had stored a chair somewhere in the bus, they were stuck on the bus. We would make arrangements for any emergency just in case of problems with bowel or bladder programs.

This seemed like a rather cruel fate, but it was reality and the players and I worked it out fairly well.

So, there they would sit.

As I walked down the aisle back to the player who had this deal for me, I wasn't anticipating anything in particular.

This was about to change!

I was about to enter into another world, another dimension of handicapped.

The world of catherization was about to rear its head.

I was about to experience, first hand, that for some people going to the bathroom is a happening. It is hourly, daily, monthly, yearly, and lifetime—day and night. It is there, male or female.

When I reached Tusa, a big 6'4" former able-body basketball player, until he wrapped his car around a telephone pole one night after finishing a season of outstanding basketball play at an area Community College, he handed me a plastic container with a handle and a lid, which locked over the spout. I was aware Bob was a very high para, a T_5-T_6. Other than this bit of information I had little idea what this really meant.

I also knew from some of the other guys that Bob drove his car using a cut-off broom handle to accelerate and break. According to the gossip he just hated the thought of driving and depending on hand-controls. I think this is illegal, but to each his own!

I should have known something was going on from the shit-eaten grin on his face and from some snickers from others seating around him.

That should have given me a clue.

I didn't take the container right away, instead asking about what kind of deal did he have for me.

He continued to grin and poke that damn container up in my direction.

"I need this dumped," he said and was now smiling—a smile that suggested he was having fun, at my expense.

"Wonderful," I replied, "dump it."

I was beginning to really understand the situation.

"It's urine, you know, piss," he informed me, "and since I can't get up and off the bus or back to the toilet to dump it, guess what, this leaves you or somebody else. Hell, you AB's ought to be worth something or be of some value."

I did know something about the situation. I don't want to appear all dumb.

I knew that for people with spinal cord injuries that result in paralysis, most have some kind of bladder dysfunction, requiring that they deal with urination in a different way. A procedure known as catherization where a tube is inserted into the urethra up into the bladder is used. As the urine flows out the tube, it is collected into a leg bag, which is strapped, to the leg. This leg bag must be drained several times a day.

I also had heard some of the guys bragging about the length of the tube inserted up into the bladder. My understanding is that most of the tubes are anywhere from six to ten inches, but the story would go that many of theirs were more towards ten to sixteen inches. But males do tend to exaggerate and tend to be big time liars on this subject.

I was still standing in the aisle and thinking, hell, when I want to take a leak, I just find the closest friendly urinal or that not being handy, a tree, wall, alley or anything that I can hide behind and get the job done. But the older I get the more frequent this has become and I might add the less controlled.

As the old saying goes, what goes around comes around.

I took the container, which was rather heavy, indicating its fullness. I walked to the back of the bus to the bathroom. Emptied it into the commode and flushed. I gotta tell you, the smell was strong. After several hours in a leg bag, wow. There is nothing quite like it and you never forget it.

Over the years I was to become very familiar with this smell. The nose knows!

As I emptied the container, I splashed some of the urine on my hand—yuck. Soap and water took care of most to this but I learned to take a pair of gives along with me to perform the task. Believe it or not sometimes people miss the container when they empty out their leg bags spilling urine on the floor, themselves and on the container and all kinds of yucky possibilities.

What I did learn was to prove very valuable. In the future I would take some uninitiated, inexperienced student manager with me on trips and assign them this wonderful, inspiring duty. A great way to relate or to bond.

This may not be fair, a bit of dirty pool if you prefer, but it was effective.

The world of catheters and leg bags, I learned they were unique to say the least.

Every time, to this day when I hear, "Boy, do I have a deal for you," I cringe.

He Can Feel It.

I shall never forget that blood-curdling scream.

We were loading a bus for a weekend trip. It was early Saturday morning. The bus was not user friendly to folks using wheelchairs. It was, therefore, not user friendly to those of us responsible for loading the bus.

It was a regular, over-the-road, 45-passenger cruiser leased from a local company. It was definitely not accessible.

Student managers to the rescue. I would work hard to find two students to travel with me. When I say hard, how about cajole, threaten, and sometimes exhausting these methods with no success, beg for help.

Sitting up in my office reflecting back on my involvement, I have often thought about the countless body and wheelchair lifting up and down stairs, up and down buses, and heavens knows what else, I'm now 5'10" whereas thirty years ago I was 6'1". Just kiddin'. But a hell of a lot of lifting.

Two, young, strong managers were an absolute necessity. And the lifting was done in whatever method it took to get the job done. The loading pattern was simple enough. Any one who could walk got on the bus first and usually went to the back seats. Those who were semi-ambulatory went next, some with and some without any help. Last would be the players in wheelchairs. They got to sit up in the front of the bus; didn't have to carry them as far. Clever? No, just back saving. Shorter distance to lift.

Figured this out rather quickly.

Loading for trips was one of my more favorite pastimes, especially if it were raining or cold and snowing.

No matter what type of transportation, bus, car, train, or air, there was sameness about the sequence and method.

Players would transfer or be carried to their seats. I, or a student manager would then take the person's wheelchair and either fold it or break it down before storing it. The players who could walk would always help. There was then the luggage, equipment, and tools, etc., that had to be packed into spaces that always seemed not designed to hold such diversity.

And of course if we loaded, we got to unload. This could be repeated several times on a specific trip with ten or more times in a two or three day period.

All of this and one more neat thing. Wheelchair use grease to lubricate their bearings and this grease invariably was transferred to my clothes. Old Levis became standard attire. Pinched fingers, abrasions, and lacerated hands was just a bonus.

I always was a whiner and expected people to feel sorry for me. But not this group. One player remarked that, "I would get my reward in heaven." Not only are they disabled but smart assess as well.

I never quite got the hang of who to load first, the big folks while I was fresh or the itty-bitty ones, saving my strength and mental set to tackle the brutes. It was usually first come, first serve or in other words, chaos.

To load an individual onto the bus, they would push up to the door. An over-the-road bus has very narrow doors with at least two steps. There is then a divider at the top of the steps, which separates the entrance from the first two seats.

This meant, that to lift someone up into the bus, the lift involved a difficult ascent up the narrow steps and then a hard ninety-degree turn at the divider and down the aisle. And the aisle is even narrower than the steps area. No problem for an able-body person, but to lift a human up this passage is an absolute bitch.

And of course the human engineering doesn't stop at this. Add a tall, high para, say six foot or better with legs that seem to be eighty-percent of his body mass, I offer for anyone serious consideration that this presents a fundamental geometrical problem. Much like putting that square peg into the round hole.

I prayed for walkers and semi-ambulatory players!

OK, time for a lift. Once the player had positioned them self at the door, the student manager and I would make a fireman carry cradle as we slipped our hands and arms underneath the player. We would thus be on either side of the player. We could then lift the player clean out of the chair. O'yes, if we had really done it correctly, the chair would be open, toward the bus so the chair does not obstruct our movement into the bus. Of course we never made this mistake requiring us to kick, shove and curse the chair out of the way, all the while trying to balance the player. We didn't really want to drop our little darling.

Once the student manager and I had secured our victim, err-player, and had lifted them out of the chair, one of us would pivot, and begin walking backward toward the bus door. At the door we would have to reach back with one foot to find the first step all the while balancing this poor soul, who would always be giving us encouragement and orders, such as, "be careful'" "watch your step," "up, up, step up," to which usually brought a very sensitive and sincere reply on my part, "Shut up Godammit." Some did, some didn't.

Trust me, I would never want to drop a poor soul, especially if they were one of my real good players.

Just kiddin'.

In this awkward fashion we would proceed up into the bus, make our right angle turn all the while having to fight the zillions of entanglements that the legs of the players, our arms and elbows, and feet seemed somehow to find. There seemed to be a law or a metabolic radar system due a spinal cord injury to seek out any and all entanglements.

Then, delicately and very gently we would swing the player over the seat arm-rest into the nearest front seat. The bigger the player the more up front they usually got to sit. On any number of occasions I would hear, "But I want to sit in the back," to which I would reply, sarcastically, "Be my guest."

We did do this maneuver as well as we could as any bouncing on something hard could have terrible consequences on the rear-end skin of the person, producing open sores, skin breakage which sometimes was very slow to heal, so there was a serious side.

Next.

It was during one of these lifts involving one rather ponderous player and I'm being kind, believe me. A better description would be heavy, heavy, obese, and fat.

We lifted him out of the chair with no apparent problem although my back would seriously argue this point. Ever want a crane? Hey, we are talking big.

I was about to learn something once again in the next few moments, something rather profound. It seems like this bundle of joy was post-polio. No big deal, right?

Wrong.

I was in the lead position and as I tried to back up the first step, the toughest part of the journey, I slipped and we almost dropped him as I lurched forward.

Notice, I said almost.

As we had lifted him out of his chair, he had wrapped his arms around our shoulders and necks and had actually clasped his hands together pulling the student manager and I together in a nose-to-nose configuration. He was so frightened about leaving the security of his chair he clung to us in a death grip. Ours.

When I slipped he tightened his hold on our heads. What's closer than nose to nose?

Whatever it is, we were.

Simultaneously, his butt, one of the tiniest parts of him, dropped down through the firemen carry and his little polio legs flew open. We were staggering under the weight and the awkward position but did catch him as we struggled to regain control. He was yelling at us in most uncomplimentary terms.

As we physically bounced him back up into our carry, his legs were still open and his testicles, yep, testicles, evidently dropped down between them.

This was the blood-curdling scream as we, in regaining our original position, squeezed his legs together catching, like a vise, these most precious body parts.

To this day I retain some deafness. God he screamed. I mean screamed.

We staggered, but completed his loading as he continued to moan and utter references to our mother's background.

Afterwards, all three of us made an inventory. No apparent structural damage.

He continued to moan. After a bit I looked at him and said, "What are you yelling about, you can't feel anything?"

"Like hell," he hissed.

I'd heard of phantom pain for amputees, but from post-polios?

He, very sarcastically, informed me that the polio virus destroys the motor cells of the spinal cord, but leaves the sensory intact, ergo (and he used ergo) a person will lose the motor function but retain the sensory. In other words, he informed me, even though he couldn't move a part, he could feel it. Then he muttered something softly, but loud enough for me to hear, "Dumb-ass PE Major."

There is no reason to doubt as to the authenticity and accuracy of such a claim.

None whatsoever!

Actually, I was just testing him to see if he knew.

Ah, the joys of road trips.

David was one of the first to reply to my request to write about being a Bronco:

My first experience with any wheelchair sports was at freshmen orientation when my Residence Assistant said let's go down and shoot some buckets. Right, I sat directly under the basket and threw the ball up as hard as I could and couldn't even touch the bottom of the net no matter the rim or consider making a shot. I never did become a scoring machine at SSU (SMSC) or since in the wheelchair teams I have been on but I have developed my skills and have come to love wheelchair sports of all kinds.

In those years there were two kinds of 'wheelchair athletes,' One. The late disabled, the car, swimming, Viet Nam, etc that took a normal' developed person and put them into a wheelchair and the early ones, the birth defects and early post polios like me that did not grow up in a world where sports were played during the growing years. So my first experience with any form of competitive sports as an active player came in college. In fact I had not even been allowed to take a PE class in high school for as I was told, "A person in a wheelchair can not compete in sports." I confronted the person that told me that by wearing my SMSC letterman jacket into his office several years later.

But because I did not grow up playing sports, when I first started, I like others, did not know what the key was or a two-one-two but that was just one of the things we all learned. Today many wheelchair programs have junior teams for ages 8–18 that allows this early opportunity to learn competitive sports.

Wheelchair sports not only providers an excellent opportunity for physical activity but also for overall improvement of health, and that right there is an outstanding benefit of all activity.

When In Doubt, Change Your Practice Area.

As part of our track and field efforts, we practiced the wheelchair field events (shotput, discus, javelin, and one I was unfamiliar with, the club throw) in a small courtyard between the physical education building and the main academic building. The courtyard was grassed and provided us with enough throwing room.

There were some obstacles—a few small pine trees, but we could angle our throws to miss them, most of the time. It was amazing the number of javelins and discus that were eaten by these trees, much like Charlie Brown's kite eating tree.

The physical education building was brick, but the main academic building was a series of vertical plate glass panels the full length of the courtyard. It didn't take a brain surgeon to figure out which way to throw.

The redeeming feature of the area was that it was located close to the physical therapy area where we stored our equipment. We would load up the shotputs, discus, javelins, and clubs into a little red radio flyer wagon.

The track and field events were rather complicated, at least for me. There were different weights and sizes depending on the level of injury, lighter and smaller for individuals with the more severe levels of injury. There was a classification system to determine what size of implement was to be used for each athlete...and...and...anyway lots of variations.

There were some athletes, in the quadriplegia and cerebral palsy classes that had trouble grasping the club, so we devised a technique where we would literally jam the small part of the club between the first two fingers of the throwing hand. Did I describe the club? Probably not. This was a new event to me, but the club throw was an event for higher and more severely disabled athletes—the club being just that, a club, smaller and lighter than a bowling pin.

To throw, the athlete, with the club between the fingers, would begin to wind-up, swinging the club at arms length several times to create momentum and to gain a rhythm, releasing it on the third or fourth swing.

This seemed to be working well until one day something happened that was a new experience for me.

I was in the courtyard working with one of our athletes, a young male, cerebral palsied. He was a new kid, one I was unfamiliar with in terms of neurological pattern or skill level. He had practiced with the discus and shotput and was going to try the club.

I explained the technique and sequence to him. I was satisfied that I had 'covered all the bases' and after placing the club in his fingers stepped back and began to count—one, two, three.

On three as instructed he attempted to throw. All of a sudden the club was flying back, towards me. The kid had not been able to release the thing, wrapping his arm around his head. This evidently triggered the release and back it came, towards me. A missile with no guidance system.

I heard him yell, "Duck!"

I ducked!

The plate glass panel didn't!

Ever try to explain something you don't understand? Especially to several administrators whose only real thought is the bottom line—who pays for the panel?

In the end, I think the University chalked it up to another Lew Shaver episode.

O'yes, we did change our practice area.

Mama Shaver Didn't Raise No Fool.

During my first couple of years, my education about the world of the 'disabled' continued. And while it did people were having a good time at my expense—and lack of knowledge, experience and awareness I might add. Babe in the woods.

One classic example of this learning process happened during one of our early track and field trips. As I recall it was to Davenport, Iowa for regional competition. Our students could qualify to advance to national competition.

This competition was separate from our basketball efforts. It was sanctioned by a national governing organization, the National Wheelchair Athletic Association. It included several classifications of quadriplegia and paraplegia groups in order to equalize competition. There was competition in swimming, weightlifting, archery, table tennis as well as various track and field events. These were all included in the regional competition.

This competition allowed some disabled individuals who due their physical limitations could not participate in wheelchair basketball an opportunity to participate against like or similar disabilities and more varied and meaningful competition.

We had taken a rather large group, some twenty-plus athletes. There were also three, additional university staff and two student managers as part of our total compliment. We had traveled by an over-the-road, forty-seven passenger bus; that meant some lifting people on and off the bus. Thus the need for extra assistance. Brute force.

We stayed in a local motel that I had been assured was 'accessible.'

Back at the motel after our first day of competition I got a phone call from John Schatzlein, informing me that it was time for one of the quads bowel program. Since it was about ten o'clock or so at night, I suggested that this was nice and wished the quad well. John insisted I did not understand, that help was required. So, I agreed to do whatever I could.

I was well aware that a well-established bowel program is an important part of a spinal cord injured persons' routine on a regular basis. Minimizes the chances for embarrassing accidents, known as an involuntary, shitting in ones pants.

I was also aware that these programs were done at a specified time and day and could involve a stimulating process to relax the bowel in order that it would then empty. I had picked up this much from over hearing conversations between various individuals on the subject, but had paid no particular attention. Actually, it was not only the extent of my knowledge, but to be truthful about all I really cared to know.

I had been given a room number and upon arrival found it full of people. This should have alerted me to something. I made my way in with a great deal of deference to my arrival. I was ushered into the bathroom.

The first thing I noticed was that the bathroom door had been removed. John informed me that this was necessary to allow a wheelchair to roll into the bathroom. When the door is on its hinges a wheelchair could not enter, so what the hell, take off the door, right?

'And what to my wondrous eyes did I see', not eight tiny reindeer, but sitting in his au-natural state, naked, was this tall, male, quadriplegic. He was sitting on a special toilet seat, which raises a person off the regular commode, a couple of inches or so. It also is open in the front. I remember turning around to exit, but of course this was not going to happen. The masses had closed ranks behind me.

Everyone was giggling, or just grinning at the situation. I knew I had been had but didn't know just how much until I was handed, no, presented with a latex glove. "Right or left handed," I was asked. After recovering from a near feint as I realized what reality actually was, I put on the glove—on my right hand. I was protesting. Good name for begging, that this was not in my job description.

To no avail. The beat went on. I was told to hold up my index finger and something called KY Jelly was spread over the finger.

I remember, very distinctly, thinking, "O'my God."

The fun continued. At least their fun. All this time Keith, the quad, just sat there, no emotion, no nothing. I was instructed to kneel down in front of Keith. Again, he was a tall drink of water, about six-four who had hurt his neck in a diving accident, which left him paralyzed from rather high in the neck region. He was classified as a C^5C6 quadriplegic.

Keith took over from this point. He told me to insert my index finger up, into his rectum. This was the finger with the jelly on it. Talk about no place for modesty!

I heard John's voice behind me, "It's called a digital, Lew."

I don't think this helped me any in the task at hand. All the specific technique and physiological aspects are lost to me over the millennium, but I recall it sometimes takes up to fifteen minutes or more of stimulation before the actual bowel movement occurs. And brother, when it does!!

For some minutes there I was in front of Keith with a real scenic view of his 'privates' staring me in the face. And I continued making little circular motions up in his rectum with my finger. Keith told me this was the technique. I couldn't believe I was doing this.

When the bowel relaxed, there was a rush of material and what a view I had of it all. I cleaned up as quickly as I could. I left Keith to shower and finish his program with someone else's help.

I received a grand round of applause when the bowel released. Real funny people. The remarks about helping several others were lost on me and comforting to know I was wanted.

Out of this experience came two important outcomes.

The first outcome was that this was definitely my second digital—the first and last!!!!!

The second was the birth of Shaver's Law. To wit—People traveling with the team in the future had to be independent, at least where bowel and bladder programs were concerned.

Hey, as I always said, "Mama Shaver didn't raise no fool." Most of the time!

4

The Dog and Pony Show

Damn Bunch Of Cripples.

After about four weeks of practice I scheduled our first game. In reality Schatzlein scheduled it through the team he played on up in Twin Cities area for a couple years. This was the only other wheelchair team in the state of Minnesota. They called themselves the Minneapolis Wheelchair Sportsman Club (MWSC). They were coached and administered by a Dr. Jim Bowen. John had gone home up in the Minneapolis area, called Dr. Bowen and scheduled a game. It had to be on a Wednesday night because that's when they practiced plus according to Dr. Bowen, the team would not travel to Marshall. So it was play in the Cities area or not play at all. We wanted to play. John was authorized to make the final arrangements and when he returned to school the Monday before the game, it was a done deal.

I had to scramble to make arrangements for transportation, travel money, and borrow game jerseys from the varsity. With a great deal of help from Glenn Mattke, the A.D., we put together two state station wagons plus a Ford van to carry the wheelchairs.

The game was scheduled for seven-thirty. That meant we needed to leave by about one in the afternoon for the three-hour trip, plus time to eat a pregame meal.

On the 27th of November, in the year of our Lord 1969, we began our very first trip to play another wheelchair basketball team. We were pumped. At least I was pumped.

The other student in addition to John Schatzlein, who was instrumental in my involvement in wheelchair sports was Curt Kettner. Curt was a post-polio, about six feet tall with really skinny legs due to the polio. One night for some reason he saw my little legs and always kidded me about my legs being as skinny as his and I hadn't even had polio. Thus for years was born the teams joke about Lew's 'polio legs.' I told him my dad used to say that the Shaver's were like potatoes with legs, thus I could blame genetics. Curt liked that.

On this occasion He was involved in one of my early and vivid memories as a wheelchair basketball coach. As I have shared with you, we were loading the van and the two wagons for this very first wheelchair game against another wheelchair team. We were heading to the Minneapolis-St. Paul area.

And again it was November. I was bundled up in my heaviest coat with a hood and had thermal gloves. It was bitterly cold with a wind blowing. My first real experience with a Minnesota 'wind chill factor.' I had the team meet me in front of the college at noon to begin loading as I was not sure what or how much time it was going to take us to get ready. After about an hour of loading wheelchairs, getting my fingers pinched in the chairs when I folded them wrong and in a general state of frustration and fatigue I looked down at Curt, who was sitting in one of the cars with a window partially down and said something to the effect that, "It took four men and a boy just to get you guys out on the road." He looked up at me and replied, "Yeah, damn bunch of cripples."

At the time I don't think I grasped the significance of his reply, I was sweating like a proverbial pig and really second guessing myself about all this. Enough said. Years later in a taped interview Curt would share with me, "…Having had polio at age nine, I grew up feeling I had been cheated…not being able to participate in sports…magnifying the feeling of being less…After enrolling at southwest State and starting to compete in wheelchair basketball, my view of life started to change…the experience gave me courage to set goals for myself and complete these goals, knowing now that the hard work and discipline that I learned from playing wheelchair basketball could carry through my life."

The First Game Reflections.

We did not return to campus until well after midnight. As I recall it was close to three. Our first game was history. I'm not sure what I really remember, the moment-to-moment things that one would think to recall. It isn't that way at all. We won, that I remember.

I called the local newspaper and the campus paper the next day and their version is as accurate as it's going to get. I would enjoy regaling anyone with my brilliant coaching strategy and on-court adjustments. The truth is I don't remember.

Rich Ousky, writing for the local *Marshall Independent*, reported that "…Shaver, the coach of the Southwest State Wheelchair basketball team, found some difficulties in the team's first game Wednesday night. He had to officiate the game…"

Yes I did. The other coach, Dr. Jim Bowen and I agreed to officiate. He explained there were no trained wheelchair officials in the area. So, he suggested and I, not knowing anything else to do, plus not being able to think of any alternative, officiated.

Ousky continued, "the team scored 10 points in the first quarter, and went on to mark up their first win rolling past the Minnesota Wheelchair Club 29–27 at Hopkins junior high school…The Twin Cities group came back to cut the Southwest lead to 13–10. Southwest led at half-time, 15–12…But in the third quarter Curt Kettner came alive and swished six points sitting down to lift the locals to a 27–18 third stanza lead."

Easy game, right? Wrong.

The article then noted, "…Southwest cooled off and their opponents got hotter outside, outscoring the locals 9–2. The other guys wheeled in close in the fourth quarter but the local bunch broke up two scoring attempts in the last 16 seconds to win by a spoke…Kettner scored eight to lead the local wheelers. Jim Stuewe added seven, plus nine big rebounds and Dan Guetter popped in six and pulled down eight caroms…Neutgens netted and grabbed four each. Schatzlein and Tusa hit for a single basket and gathered in seven and six rebounds, respectively. Pete Hansen failed to make the scoring column but contributed several fine passes.

The College newspaper, *The Impact*, whose reporter is lost to me, put it this way, "Two quarters of fast break, 1–2–2 zone basketball propelled Southwest's rehabilitation—student cagers to a 29–27 victory over Minneapolis' Wheelchair Sportsman Club at Hopkins last Wednesday…We looked good in two quarters and slowed down the other two, commented Shaver…"

We only called four fouls in the game, but at times it was more like demolition derby, but I sure didn't understand the game enough to really control it. The Minneapolis group was 'bangers', wheel-to-wheel, elbow-to-elbow and my team didn't back off. I suppose if you talked to Jim Bowen he might tell you we were the 'bangers'. This was to be the first of several meetings between our two groups and I'm not sure it got too much better; would like to think it did.

And finally, Ousky commented, "Lew has some problems with terminology…He likes to see his men run with the ball but they can't. It's illegal for them to get out of their chairs…When you're yelling at a group of wheelers it's hard to distinguish between fast break and fast brake."

To say I had a lot to learn would be a gross understatement. Kettner told me to play the 1–2–2 Zone. He told me it was what he played out in Denver, the idea being to deny the offense any inside shots. Seemed to work rather well, at least against our initial opponents. I was yet to learn of the shortcomings later, but for now, whatever works. We made the sports page, which was important. The team did mention us being referred to as 'rehabilitation-student cagers which didn't set too well.

But, hey, we had number one under our belt, we won our first ball game.

Our First Tournament.

Rich Ousky of the *Marshall Independent* continued to report our play throughout the remaining part of the season. Under the title SPORTS SHOTS he wrote, "The Southwest State Broncos wheelchair basketball team is developing a program in which there will be a number of winners and hopefully few if any losers. Lew Shaver, coach and general manager of the Broncos, said he hopes the team can schedule a number of benefit games next year that will serve a host of purposes. The games will be exhibitions of what people with handicaps can do. They will also provide the Broncos with funds for traveling expenses that will enable them to play other games. Most important, the games will raise funds for purposes worthwhile and specifically to the Bronco team. The Broncos will split the proceeds from the games 60–40. Forty percent will go to the Broncos and the larger half will go to the sponsors of the games on the condition that it be used for or donated to rehabilitation-type programs…Shaver said he has hopes of making a trip next year that would take the Broncos to two or three spots where they could meet more established college wheelchair teams…

Our crowning achievement, beyond survival, of this first year came in a tournament sponsored by a medical company of the Twin Cities area and Courage Center, a rehabilitation program and facility located in Golden Valley, a suburb north of the cities. There were to be four teams. Besides us in the tournament, there were the MWSC, a team from Abbey Rents (able-bodied) and a team of camp counselors from Camp Courage (also able-bodied). The site was Camp Courage, located northwest of the cities in Maple Lake. Camp Courage is a camp for disabled youngsters of all disabilities designed for recreational and therapeutic purposes sponsored by Courage Center.

On April 10th and 11th, 1970, we did battle.

The Marshall Independent in bold headlines, on the sports page proclaimed SMSC'S BRONCOS WIN FIRST STATE WHEELCHAIR TOURNEY. My all time favorite was how the College paper announced, again in bold letters, CHAIRED CAGERS CROWNED CHAMPS at CAMP COURAGE. Great, great alliteration.

We had made history. We won the very first state or for that matter any team athletic championship. Let me repeat, we had won THE first championship for the college in athletics. Yep, we tooted our horn a bit, or at least I tooted my horn a bit.

We beat our one and only wheelchair foe of the year, MWSC, 27–25 in the championship game after beating the guys from Abbey Rents 49–30. This was our third two-point victory over them. We sandwiched a 48–46 win in between this win and our first ever win.

Reflections of the First Year.

At the end of my first season, my thoughts were very similar to when I completed my first year of, say college, or teaching. I think this is especially true of the teaching experience. Very few textbooks or academic pursuits can prepare a person for all the ins'n outs of any job. The basics are there, but the day-to-day, intra-organizational, and all the personality intricacies can overwhelm a person. After a period of time there must be a comfort zone that is achieved if one is to be successful. This can happen quickly or can take even years I suspect.

I was fortunate. I enjoyed teaching from the get-go and coaching was like icing on the cake.

Maybe because I had so much to learn, my first season was what? Awesome comes to mind. It was certainly challenging, not having much of a background. Prosthetics and orthotics were not a part of my previous education. And rehabilitation was probably just some word, a very nondefinition if you will. I was just a word without any true meaning or understanding.

The old cliché about 'learning more than you taught' was rather appropriate in my case.

The season was rather short on competition. We only played four true wheelchair games, all against the team from the Minneapolis-St. Paul area, winning all four. But I counted all our games including the ten benefit or exhibition games and claimed our record to be 14–0. Hey, sounds better than 4–0. The highlight of the season had to be, one, we survived, and number two, winning the first ever athletic championship at Southwest. This still makes for a good trivia question.

Let's see, what did I learn or become aware of specifically? That would be a book unto itself, but there were several things that do come to mind.

After the incident at the restaurant, someone back in our rehab program told me I had experienced a classic example of the 'Theory of Spread.' It goes something like this. If an individual has a disability of one kind or another, in this case, having to use a wheelchair then the 'total' human must also be disabled. Therefore, people in wheelchairs are also mentally retarded and that was why the waitress spoke to us in 'baby talk.' We were mentally retarded. I suspect it is more complicated than this, but it will do for my understanding.

It was also pointed out that another situation occurred. When we came in the restaurant, the adults acted like we were not there, they would not stare. I thought it was because they were uncomfortable or just being polite. Nope, it was suggested we were 'invisible'. We were not there. We, in essence did not exist. It was suggested to me that this is a form of denial. If it ain't there it can't or won't affect or hurt us. We therefore do not deal with it. Wow. One individual in the rehab program pointed out, in her opinion, this is the way we deal with many issues, such as racial, religious, illness, and so forth. Pretend it or they aren't there. No problem, right?

The most basic thing I began to learn had to do with dealing with the person in a wheelchair I was becoming very much aware that the wheelchair does not define the individual. It wasn't too long into the season I noticed that not all people in chairs like each other, that some are real 'pains in the ass' while others are really neat individuals. Sounds like normal, right? I know this is what is taught and what should be. Treat them as I would treat anyone else. But I found myself doing the opposite from time to time. One week or so I would be me as a coach and the next week I would try to 'relate to each player', which is fine as a theory, but it wound up for me 'trying to be all things to all people.' I think this is a recipe for failure. A colleague once shared with me, he couldn't guarantee success, but he could guarantee failure, trying to please everyone. You wind up pleasing nobody. What a thought and one I that wrestle with from time to time.

There were differences. One example involved travel, the loading and unloading. It was a happening. I had to allow for extra time. To be even more specific, one player had a bowel routine that had to be done after his evening meal. This took at least thirty minutes or so. I found myself finishing my meal and ready to leave on several trips, only to be reminded that so 'n so was in the 'can doing his bowel program.' Patience is not one of my virtues, but when nature calls or to be more accurate, when nature has to do what nature does, not much anyone can do.

I also felt I had found something that was really unique and rewarding. The players were playing for the right reasons, no one was paying them, our crowds were rather small, usually some friends a few family members. This was true at home and certainly true on the road. People have a hard time equating athleticism to a wheelchair according to many of the players. We were equated with Special Olympics many times.

The First Intercollegiate Game.

The University of Illinois. The Holy Grail for Intercollegiate Wheelchair sports.

If this seems a bit exaggerated or blasphemes, I don't mean for it to come off this way. There is usually a place and/or a person in any field or area that is considered as the center of knowledge.

In the fall of 1969, my first year at Southwest, The University of Illinois was already celebrating some twenty-plus years of programming for the disabled. I, for one was in awe.

Twenty-plus years!!

Neither I, nor probably anyone can really give the proper due to the Illinois program for its revolutionary efforts on behalf of the disabled after World War II. And one man must, in my humble opinion, be singled out—Tim Nugent. This mans' vision and his efforts are an absolute legend in the field of rehabilitation education.

I suspect that for the greater population at large, Tim remains in splendid anonymity, only known within a rather small group of people. He has had a profound effect throughout the world. The University of Illinois is renown for the variety and depth of academic, athletic, and physical and educational support programs for the disabled population.

In any case, our rehabilitation program at Southwest owed much to Tim. Early in the fall of 1969, myself, because I was coaching wheelchair basketball, and two others from Southwest were flown down to the University of Illinois campus in Champaign-Urbana, to visit the Rehabilitation-Education Center and observe the programs.

The other two were our university nurse and our physical therapist. We had the daunting task to coordinate in the development of a Federal Grant to secure start up monies for the program at Southwest. We spent two or three days touring the campus in general and specifically the Center itself. We talked to the staff and the faculty within the program. To say we were impressed with the facilities and the educational support programs would not do justice to my personal impression.

The most impressive time was the time we spent with Tim himself. He talked. We listened. He philosophized. We cataloged. He envisioned. We dreamed.

We left with our heads reeling. We left with a sense of purpose and a definite direction. We completed and were awarded the Grant later in the year.

I was duly impressed. I can only hope Tim would be proud of our efforts at Southwest.

I returned about a year later. It was December 3, 1970. This would be the first intercollegiate wheelchair basketball game in the history of the sport.

Tim and Stan Labanowich, the coach of the Illinois' wheelchair team had spent the better part of this day sharing their considerable knowledge and expertise.

They made themselves available to answer my many questions. They also gave our team a tour of the Rehabilitation-Education Center with all its services and support programs.

My kids were impressed. The wheelchair repair services was one particular area which was awe inspiring. This service could machine and repair any wheelchair or specific part. It had the capacity to actually build a chair.

Our game chairs were run-of-mill street model chairs. They probably weighed about sixty pounds, were wide, big, and not modified for sport performance. But that's all we had. It was evident Tim and Stan felt sorry for us and offered to let us play in a few of their competitive chairs. Wow, from huge, German Tiger Tanks to competitive chairs.

It was early Christmas for my team. Talk about faster and quicker.

We accepted their offer in a heartbeat.

This aspect of sportsmanship has always impressed me about the people in wheelchair sports. Not all of them, some are real dinks, but there is a unique camaraderie that I haven't found in other sports arenas. People share with a real quality. They are willing to share their techniques and knowledge about modification and all aspects of the game. What is most impressive to me was that there were few professional people involved in the sport, most were volunteers.

An excellent example of this lies in the national governing body of the sport, The National Wheelchair Basketball Association; its all volunteer from its Executive Committee, Commissioner, to the working committees down to the various coaching and team management at the regional and local levels.

And no federal government money. None. Self sustaining. Remarkable in my opinion. I think it is the single largest wheelchair sports association with about 2,000 members.

Each year, all association issues are completed at the NWBA version of the Final Four. A local or regional group hosts the national tournament. Each team within the organization is allocated two delegates to the meeting held in conjunction with the tournament. An ambitious task. It works, for over fifty years. Budgetary, playing rules and regulations and various administrative issues are considered in a two or three day period.

Tim was one of the founding fathers and is generally credited with the majority of the original idea and resulting organization. He served as the first commissioner for the first twenty-five years. Stan was the second commissioner.

Any wonder I was excited to be a part of this history and a bit in awe? To be a part of the growth and development involved in the first intercollegiate game was a personal high. All the other teams in the NWBA were community teams, not university oriented, so Illinois had had no intercollegiate competition these many years.

As a matter of fact, they had won the national championship in 1969, the previous year, and had four starters returning from this team. This is what made them different from all the other teams in the sport. Players graduated as opposed to the rest of the teams whose players could and did play for years and years. This was a powerful team we were about to play.

In my youthful exuberance and as I look back, my lack of understanding, I was almost cocky in thinking that a Lew Shaver coached team was going to compete on this level. It was a challenge. You gotta' believe.

We were scared, but excited as hell; at least I was!!!

We scored the first four points to lead 4–0. I was feeling pretty good, even confident that, hell maybe this wasn't going to be all that difficult.

Then Illinois came away with a defensive rebound. I saw Stan nod yes to one of his players as they brought the ball up the court.

I was about to find out what that little nod meant.

It meant unleash the dogs.

Press.

Attack.

I will save myself some agony and share the final score: Illinois 46—Southwest 6.

Yep, six.

That's not the total story in all this. Important, you bet, but not the real part of this picture.

When the score reached something like 16–4, Tim eased up behind me down on our bench, pulled me aside, and told me to follow him upstairs to the balcony seating above the floor.

That's correct, he took me. I protested. I needed to be with my team on the bench. They needed me.

Tim simply informed me I would learn more up above with him.

Who was I to argue? I was a bit miffed at being treated like some rookie. I did swallow my pride and ego and followed him. Under protest, but silently. Surly, but silently.

He also instructed me to bring paper, pencil, and a clipboard.

Please understand, I had been in coaching for some ten years at the high school level prior to going to Southwest. It was not like I had no experience. And here was this, this…person, treating me like…what? I guess I was embarrassed. It was unique to say the least. But he insisted I follow him.

I did.

I went.

I saw.

I didn't conquer. I did learn—from a master. Kicking and silently screaming all the way. An incredible experience. One I shall not forget.

Tim came down at halftime and shared some of his observations with my kids. After halftime we were back upstairs.

I would substitute by yelling down to the bench.

Both Tim and Stan joined us back at the motel after the game. This continued my boot camp.

Stan stayed until two or three in the morning sharing his knowledge and experiences

Incredible teachers. Both of them.

Walk, My Son.

"I'm tired of sitting in this chair. I'm tired of being a cripple."

The crowd hushed.

No, the crowd sat in stunned silence. A silence, as someone once described, that shouted.

Then there was a collective gasp. A gasp of disbelief.

Did everyone really hear right? Did one of those poor crippled students really say such a thing?

My team had just completed their pregame warm-up. We were in a small southwestern Minnesota town. It was a Saturday night.

The town was similar to many in this region. It was a typical, small southwestern Minnesota farming community. As the old saying goes, "If you've seen one, you've seen them all." Just a wide spot on the road. Rural America. The grain elevator is the predominant feature as you come into town. There may or may not be one, four way stop. No lights, just a four way stop. The population is under two thousand, and sometimes under one.

The sign outside of both ends of town proclaim the state championships in the various high school sports. Sports are a primary business and an important societal focus, if not the focus. There is nearly always The Cafe on Main Street that still serves plate lunches for less than $5.00 and of course makes the best pies in the county.

The local population fight school district consolidation as this part of America tries to survive and retain its identity. These are farming and hard working people basically of Northern European stock.

Many towns retain the culture of the old country, be it Norwegian, Polish, Finish, Belgium, or German. Each is distinctive or as some might suggest, clannish. But good, hard working people.

Don't try to tell them that bigger is better when it comes to their schools. It ain't going to play.

The gym we were playing in was an older gym, a cracker-box, which provides unique obstacles for the players. This particular gym has a raised floor, theater style. The floor is a good three feet above the lower seating area. There is a balcony for extra seating.

This was a benefit game for us. We would go into a community and play local people, providing them with the five wheelchairs. It was a fund-raiser for us. The money we earned supplemented the university budget we received as part of the athletic program.

Ask any coach. Budgets are never enough.

The players and I referred to these events as our 'dog and pony' show. There was an educational aspect to our efforts in addition to fund-raising. We were trying to emphasize that. "It's ability, not disability that counts." We, or at least myself, thought this was a rather noble effort.

And while this was true, it was the money that sure helped. Sound familiar?

Around five in the afternoon, we rolled into town, packed in two station wagons, one pulling a trailer, loaded to capacity with all the chairs and equipment.

The idea of the benefit game was to come into a community, play a game against local people or groups. There would be a sponsoring group, which might include service groups of Rotarians or Kiwanis, or perhaps high school classes raising monies for prom or other specific needs. We did encourage these groups to earmark some of the money to a disability oriented activity. Just a request.

The financial terms or deal would include splitting the net proceeds fifty-fifty. This allowed the sponsors to advertise, pay for any gym rental if necessary, and any other expenses without giving us a guarantee that might make it tough to make ends meet.

Sometime we did well while other we would barely cover our own expenses. Some communities would feed us at the local cafe or in the school lunch-room as part of the deal. Whatever works.

On this night our 'opponents' would include four, separate, groups—local teachers, the high school girls' basketball team, the boys' team, and a team of local business and governance individuals.

We would modify our games playing four-eight minute quarters to allow the four groups equal time. Normally we played two-twenty minute halves under NCAA rules.

I would meet with the local players as they tried to warm up. With only five chairs and some twenty to thirty people, this presented a problem. We made do. I would discuss the rules of the game and a few common situations that might be unique to wheelchair basketball. The officials, also from the community would be invited in on this session. The old two birds with one stone.

The discussion was standard in nature. I would begin by emphasizing that wheelchair basketball is played under NCAA rules with few exceptions. I would stress only the ones that were going to impact on the local groups. These included that contact with the chair was like that of the general rules of contact in 'regular' basketball such as charging and blocking. The chair is part of the player. The dribble is done by dribbling, passing or shooting before taking no more than two pushes on the chair. Taking three pushes without doing something with the ball is traveling. I would stress that players must stay seated in the chair so that they do not gain an advantage. And out-of-bounds is simple, the wheels determine position on the floor, just as feet do in the 'regular' game.

There were always some questions and I would forget to cover something, but we would deal with that the best we could once the game began. Lets see, "Yes, there is the jump ball, but players can not jump, and yes, there is a three point shot and a free throw." I explained that at the free throw line and the three-point line was judged by the large, back wheels. This puts the shooting plane approximately the same as an "able-bodied" counterpart. Gasp, gasp.

I would ask one or two of our players to come down and demonstrate these various interpretations.

There was one, safety issue I covered. The wheelchairs that we used were modified for competition, 'chopped and channeled' for speed and quickness. The chairs had a shorter wheel base with many of the backs lowered. A platform on wheels. A hot rod machine for basketball.

The reason for this emphasis was elementary. With the modifications came a 'tippy' problem. The chair would flip over backwards when the weight shifted. Guess what would happen to any one in the chair? Yep, over they would go—backward. The technique to counter this was simply to tuck the chin to the chest and roll out of the chair. Go with the flow, don't fight city hall. By tucking the chin, I would assure the people they would land on their upper back, not on their heads.

We never lost one poor soul.

About five minutes before game time I would call our team over to the sideline and with microphone in hand step out onto the floor.

I would introduce myself, tell the audience how happy we were to be in their community, thank the sponsoring organization and say a few words about Southwest and the wheelchair program. I would share with the people how Southwest was one of only a very few universities in the world with such a program. And with no little bit of pride, I would tell them that our players were true student-athletes and our program was the only one I could identify that was a varsity sport and housed in the Athletic Department.

We would then have one of our players demonstrate the various rules of the game.

If one of our players was from the local area, I would have them do the demonstration. A sort of 'home town kid makes good.'

Before introducing my team, I would indicate to the audience that tonight, it was my opinion that he local groups were 'the handicapped' and that at the beginning of each quarter we would give each of them sixteen points and we would try to catch them.

This always brought a roar of laughter and applause.

What an ego booster!

Our players also referred to these games as 'ego trips.' A person pushing a chair for the first time and at the same time handle the ball would present a challenging evening. Our kids would literally 'run circles' around our opponents. The audience would roar in approval and laugh when one of the teachers or star ballplayers would make a fool out of themselves. Great fun.

But I wanted our players to play well, execute their moves and shots with precision. I wanted us to have fun, but to also play with a high degree of excellence. I wanted people to be in awe of the skill level of the game.

Then would come the introduction of our players. I should have smelled something was going on. Roger Olson, my student manager, had asked me prior to the warm-up if he could suit up and go through the warm up with the team.

I was busy at the time, not paying much attention and nodded OK.

In retrospect, I was a bit brain dead.

So there was Roger, just another player to the crowd.

Each individual player would be introduced. This would include their academic status and major, jersey number, position, and hometown.

Something like, "At a guard, number 22, a sophomore majoring in Business Administration, from such 'n such town, Joe Schmuck. With this, the player would roll out on the floor to thunderous applause and pivot toward the crowd.

Each, in turn would be introduced forming a straight line. And, just like the Big Guys each player would go down the line with high fives and what have you.

I had just introduced the last player, Ed, before it would be Roger's turn. Ed was a veteran who had been diagnosed with Multiple Sclerosis while in service. After discharge, he decided to come to college, no matter that MS is progressive. As he told me one day, "Hell Lew, everyone is going to die, some of us earlier than others. In the meantime I plan to enjoy life and not worry too much about it."

Something about one day at a time. Sound familiar?

"And last, but not least ladies and gentleman," I continued, "number 52, a sophomore from Fairmont, Minnesota, a Marketing Major, Roger Olson."

Out he went, down the line with high fives and lined up next to Ed at the end of the line. I turned to face the crowd after watching him take his position to say a few parting remarks when I heard the proclamation from Roger about being tired of sitting in the chair and wanting to walk.

Roger had a great gym voice and there was no one and I mean no one who did not hear him. It was a packed gym numbering almost nine hundred and I've never heard so many people so quiet.

I had no idea what was happening or what was going to happen. I suspect that more than just a few of the former players will attest that this was not so unusual.

I dropped the mike to my side in mid-sentence, turned around just in time to see Ed lay his hands on Rogers' head and loudly proclaim, "So be it my son, walk, walk, walk."

And with that, Roger got up out of his chair and walked across the floor and out of the gym through a locker room door.

Let's see. Stunned? Confused? Na, just complete disbelief.

Me and the crowd.

The rest of the team was laughing their heads off. I stood in the middle of the floor not having a clue what to do.

The crowd was with me. Not a sound.

I recovered after a few moments, and sensing what was happening tried to explain to the crowd that this was the team's way at laughing at life. At least that is what I meant to say.

I'm not sure what I did say. It must have been OK. Desperation is the invention of inspiration. My inspiration was to hand the mike to Ed and let him explain. Pass the buck when all else fails.

He talked about playing a joke on the people to have some fun and was sorry if it alarmed them. It seemed to work.

We played the game and finished the evening in grand fashion.

And Roger and Ed? They thought they were just the greatest.

It crossed my mind to shoot them both.

The antics weren't over yet. Why should I have ever thought any different?

After the introductions, there was still about two minutes until game time. I told my team just to shoot some lay ups. During the drill a basketball mysteriously appeared rolling toward the edge of the stage. Right behind it went Danny Guetter, a single leg amp, pushing his chair like crazy. Just as the ball went over the edge, well there was the ball, there was Danny. I watched. The ball. Danny. The edge of the stage.

I also saw five or six of the front rows down off the stage vacate in one mass movement. The ball went over the edge and just as it seemed Danny would follow, he rocked his chair back, grabbed one wheel, which spun him around almost 180 degrees and with inches to spare pushed back onto the court. With a big, shit eating grin on his face.

One Hundred.

One hundred, one hundred, one hundred they chanted as they pushed off the floor at half time.

I was late February during a tough year.

My team was struggling, just to survive and exist. Sometimes, just having five players, all of which had to be academically eligible and meet the classification system requirements that are a part of wheelchair basketball was a challenge. It was interesting and at times, almost impossible at worst.

Illness, surgical requirements, deaths in families and it seems like a million other reasons reduced the team from time to time, even week to week—in numbers and skill level.

This particular year had been especially difficult. To begin the season there were nine available players. A good number. This did not last long.

Mike Haig, a high level quad, tried for a couple of weeks, but found the effort to be just too much. We talked and he decided to 'hang it up' but did indicate he would help us out should an emergency arise. He thanked me for the opportunity. Said it was important for him to know his functional capabilities and limitations and that this experience was really significant.

A few weeks' later two players developed pressure sores, ulcerations on their butts. So called 'bedsores.' These can be mean, even life threatening. Each year we would review skin care issues with the players prior to the season. We had knowledgeable and professional staff of rehabilitation specialist who would discuss the issue. All our players would be cautioned that the external pressure from prolonged sitting plus the daily routine of transfer and general hygiene considerations could all play a part. This is true specifically where bony parts are close to the skin surface such as the elbows, tailbone, and where we sit under the butt area.

Somewhat true to human form, a couple of people had to be hospitalized for this reason. They both lost several months from school in the healing process.

From nine to six players in about three short weeks.

I was elated when we added another player at the start of the winter quarter in December. We were now seven strong. There was cause for jubilation.

For every reaction there is an opposite and equal reaction. Disaster struck.

In February just before making a trip to play a powerful community team, 'the sky was falling, the sky was falling.' And Chicken Little was nowhere to be found.

On Wednesday of this particular week, prior to leaving on Friday, I found out the new player, the one enrolled in December, had developed a pressure sore and was in the hospital. Please read my lips, we stressed this issue, and stressed this issue. Maybe we should have stressed it some more!

Damn. Besides being a warm body, he was also a pretty good player.

Back to six players. But, who me worry?

On Thursday, another player was hospitalized with a bladder infection.

Down to five players.

The worst was yet to come.

Thursday night another player called me on the phone at home to inform me his Grandfather had died and the funeral was over the weekend. Damn inconsiderate of the old gentleman.

I wanted to plead and the player to…what? There was no decision to be made.

The funeral was the only and the right option.

Houston, we have a problem.

The next morning, Friday, I contacted a student who had played briefly the previous year, but due to his academic major in mechanical engineering, had opted to devote his time and energies in that direction and not wheelchair basketball.

I was prepared for a no answer; he would not go with us. I was prepared for the worst, but he said he would go. In fact, he indicated, as I recall that it would be a welcome break. It saved me from a pathetic session, in public, of total prostration and out and out begging. This I was prepared to do!

I left him thinking, "Yes, we have five."

Later that morning, I happened to run into the young quad that was with us for a couple of weeks earlier in the year and invited him to go. I knew he was independent and suggested he might enjoy the trip.

He thought for a few seconds and said sure he would go.

I walked away thinking, "Yes, there is a God, but what a sense of humor He must have."

Now fast forward to Saturday. To halftime. One-hundred was still on my mind. I sat dumbfounded and not just a little bit pissed. The other team was gone by now but their chant was still with me.

The score was 50–5. We had the five if that is not obvious.

The other team had pressed us the entire first half. Twenty minutes of pure hell. It was a moral victory for my team when we crossed the ten-second line for Gods' sake.

Our opponents at this time in our history were predominantly against community teams, which are older and more experienced. They were not encumbered with eligibility rules, nor losing players to graduation. This was reality and we struggled to compete.

Hope this does not sound like complaining or whining, 'just the facts, man, just the facts.'

Watching my kids get destroyed, especially after such a shit week was really tough to take. In addition, they did not substitute. They had some fourteen players and had only played six.

Life sure is tough. And sometimes there is nothing one can do about it.

As the old saying goes, shit happens! But why us, right?

I sat on our bench for a few moments, began to gather what wits I had left, and then slowly began to make my way to our locker room.

When I came into the room, my first impression was one of silence. I have been to funerals with more noise. The kids were in shock. Deep shock.

I looked at them. They looked at me. I'm the coach and supposed to say or do something brilliant, to fix all this.

Every once in awhile my heart would tug, in a big way. Yeh, even we hard noses. Compassion is an interesting feeling for some of us.

I stood and smiled and paused. The kids waited. For the word to come down on high, or…or…or. I didn't know. Maybe a pep talk about 'win one for the Gipper,' or 'win one for good old Southwest.'

What they got was a gut reaction.

"One hundred my ass," I said in a slow and deliberate voice. This was before the advent of the shot clock in basketball. I continued, "Don't shoot. If you get trapped, bounce the ball out of bounds off their wheelchairs. Hold the ball as long as we can."

I told them I was sorry I didn't have any magic to offer. We had to do the best we could with what we had.

They seemed to understand and agreed.

Second half. It worked!!!! We played keep away long enough so that after ten minutes into the half the score was only 65–5. A moral victory. Or at least some solace to a horrible situation. They pulled their press and even substituted.

Amen.

By this time, out players were beat. With only six players there was not much wiggle room for substituting. These players got to play whether they wanted to or not.

The player I designated, as the one to throw the ball in from out of bounds finally got so tired he would park himself under the basket so that when the other team would score he would already be in position to get the ball.

Can't say I blamed him.

Towards the end of the game a ball came through the net and hit him on top of the forehead jarring his glasses catty-whampus and jarred some snuff out of his mouth that ran down his chin. I did not know he had any of this stuff. He evidently hid it well, so this came as a surprise. To me, a not so funny surprise. A pissed me off surprise.

I began to shout at him, don't remember what I was saying. At the moment, it seemed like the thing to do.

He gained control of the ball and sat, too tired to move, his glasses all over his face and that damn snuff running down his chin.

I was up off the bench and became aware of someone laughing up in behind our bench. I turned around. It was our physical therapist, who evidently had nothing better to do that weekend and made the trip with us. Actually he made several trips with yes to assist in the loading and unloading.

At his point in time I failed to find the humor in the situation.

He was laughing his buns off.

For whatever reason or reaction, this really pissed me off and I told him I didn't think it was so damn funny.

Some of us have no sense of humor.

Given all that had gone wrong and all that continued going wrong, it was probably a fitting conclusion.

You Did What With Him?

He was always a mouthy little guy. One day it caught up with him.

We had moved our game equipment, extra wheelchairs, luggage, and personal paraphernalia and what-have-you of the rehab area down to the back loading door, waiting for our bus to arrive to leave on a week trip.

We were heading for the southern part of Wisconsin and then down to Southern Illinois University at Carbondale, Illinois.

Two students were going with me as managers as this was one of the first long trips we had ever made and I was trying to play it safe. I figured I could use all the help I could get.

Both managers were pretty good-sized lads. We were going to be loading and unloading and lifting people on and off the bus two, three, maybe four times a day for some ten days. We were scheduled to play four games, two in Wisconsin over the weekend and two in Carbondale on the following Tuesday-Wednesday. Strong backs, weak minds.

I returned to the loading area after picking up sack lunches from the university food service. Sack lunches were one of our main staples and dearly loved by all.

Just kiddin'. Actually, they were a cheaper than a meal on the road. A couple of cold meat sandwiches, a piece of fruit, a bag of potato chips, and a can of pop plus packets of catsup, mayonnaise or mustard comprised this much sought after delicacy. On his long trip I had ordered twenty of the gourmet delights. I had to place the order a few days in advance. We got a break, as some of them would be freebies as a number of our players ate in the Food Service. We did not have to pay for their sack lunch as they were going to miss several meals while on the trip. I used a wheelchair to pick up the lunches as the Food Service was on the other side of campus. The chair made a good cart to stack the big boxes the lunches were packed in. Good thinking, huh?

The sack lunches also saved us time. We did not need to stop to eat. We could move on down the road for four to six hours, depending on the bus drivers' situation. On this extended trip we had two drivers—some regulations require this as I was told. Since the university was paying for this expense, it was OK with me. The first part of our trip was to be about ten to twelve hours. The drivers could drive only so many hours at one time or in a specific time frame. Anyway, there were two of them.

The arrival of the lunches always provoked comments. The rookies on the trip were in for an interesting experience. Upper class members would tell them that only one sandwich was actually theirs. Some really believed this. Rookies!!!

To supplement this royal feast, we took a large cooler to hold juice and pop. There was always the reminder to the spinal cord injured that they must maintain fluid intake and that every thirty minutes or so they needed to relieve the pressure off their butts by lifting up or laying down on their side for a brief period of time. I knew the upper class players were thrilled to hear this every time we went somewhere. Our Physical Therapist made sure I appreciated the importance of this action. He would always remind me that to disregard this advice was to invite skin problems that could lead to serious consequences. Being the good soldier I was, I obeyed. Besides the fact that I respected the Therapist knowledge he was also much bigger than I.

I tried never to be short with the sack launches, but no matter the head count and pre-trip preparation, we would sometimes be a couple short. I went hungry and worse, someone would remark something to the effect that what could they expect from a PE Major.

When the bus arrived I did not pay much attention to any of the conversations taking place between individuals. Loading all the people and their gear, plus game equipment, toolbox, etc., was about all I could handle. I also would invariably have to run back to my office or the rehab area for something or other. It got to be rather chaotic. And chaos leads to grumpiness, with a short fuse. I mean I was responsible for all this, right? And I took this very seriously. Sometimes much too serious, but that's what perfectionist do. I was intense and preoccupied.

I had developed a checklist and checked off each item as it was loaded, everything from wheelchairs, toolbox, scorebook, pencils, stat sheets, and clipboards were all checked off. And like a good Santa, I would be 'checkin' it twice.'

No matter who cold it was I would find myself sweated through during the loading. Even with two student managers loading most of the players.

No good clothes. Grease from the chairs ate good clothes. And for the ever present 'finger eating wheelchairs', I wore gloves.

Finally, loaded. I checked my office for the tenth time. I could always seem to find some item I needed to check again, somewhere. I took it as a personal affront if I forgot something. At least it would piss me off and ruin a good day.

I was on the bus letting the two managers finish up. As a matter of fact, I was having a cup of coffee, sitting in the front seat of the bus—The coaches' seat. I could drink a coffee rather freely on this trip as the bus had a bathroom in it for those of us with tiny bladders. This was a real treat. The bus was not very accessible, but by golly there was a restroom.

Pretty fair trade if you ask me.

The managers were helping the bus drivers close the underneath bay doors and the last minute checks were made as all came aboard, indicating we were ready to go.

One last check, as I huddled with the student managers and called out the items on the checklist, the managers would verify that the item was accounted for.

One last check. I wanted to see all the players. That would be the ultimate mistake.

I went down the aisle checking to make sure all were aboard.

I would call out the team roster, one player at a time. "So n' so," and a response of "here", yes, yep, or yo," would acknowledge their presence.

"So n' so,"—check.

"So n' so,"—check.

"Rider,"—no response

Again, a bit louder, "Rider." No response.

There were some rather sly, knowing smiles on the faces of a few people, and I became suspicious. On an earlier trip the upper class players had passed a freshman up over the seats all the way to the back of the bus and gagged him.

"OK, where is Rider," I demanded looking towards the rear of the bus. I repeated this question in the best command voice I had, knowing well it didn't mean shit to this group. Image is everything. Sure it is.

Shrugs, but no responses.

"Come on dammit, where is he?"

"You might want to look on the lockers just inside the door coach," volunteered another freshman.

"Shit, fellas, somebody go get him," I growled.

People were now laughing. Big joke.

As I indicated, Rider was rather a mouthy little guy. He was a post-polio, about five-foot nothing, ninety pounds soaking wet. He loved to argue and screw around.

On this day he and one of the student managers were verbally abusing each other, in a friendly sort of way, of course.

As I heard later, Rider was reminding the manager about something embarrassing that had happened to him and as some discussions of this type develop, it turned sour and I heard rather personal.

The manager finally warned him to shut up, to 'get off his case.' But the hot button had been pushed. Rider persisted.

The final insult was something that impugned the managers character or manhood or some such shit. The manager simply picked Rider bodily out of his chair and planted him on top of a row of student lockers located down the hall from the loading dock door.

Planted him and left him.

I had made my last round and was already on the bus. I had no idea what was going on. So what's new?

I looked at the manager and he simply shrugged insisting he knew nothing of this. Just a misunderstood little angel.

I motioned for him to follow me. We got off the bus and went back into the building. As I came through the door I could hear Rider screaming and rounding the corner to the lockers we found him still perched, like a cupie doll, on top of the lockers.

He saw me and began yelling about some SOB Able-body fink who had left him and worse, had taken his chair.

I think he was a bit miffed.

When he says the manager, he repeated some of his ranting with a few choice additions, which were returned by the manager in spades.

I told them both to please shut up. I say told, kinda like asking, but much more firmer.

I let them settle down a few moments, then asked the manager to please get him down and carry him back to the bus. I looked up at Rider and asked him to calm down so we could get on our way.

Down he came and over the shoulder he went like a sack of potatoes. As they went around the corner to the door, I heard the manager say something to the effect that if he undid his suspenders, he would find himself in the nearest snow bank.

Never ends.

Like two, naughty children, I made them sit as far apart on the bus as possible for a while. I did ask the manager if he would have let us leave without him. He just smiled.

End of problem. Not really. Evidently the dispute a continued. Twice more on this trip I found Rider in a snow bank outside the bus as we were loading.

Put Me In Coach.

"Ramier, take your jacket off," I informed the player sitting next to me.

I was ready to substitute. My first five was stinking up the floor. Poor shooting, turnovers, and just plain brain-dead mistakes! We were winning the game, but only by a few points.

My coaching philosophy has always been to let the team work out of such situations. I had been running the sideline, yelling, screaming, encouraging and all the terms or words of endearment of course. I had even invoked the Lords' name a few times to perhaps increase our chances of success. Surprise, surprise. Nothing was working.

For a coach it is a frustrating situation, at least to this coach. For me, the archetypical Type A personality, anal in many areas of life, it was frustrating and intense. But I do love it!

One player, who was privileged to sit by me, when I sat, for a couple of years told his parents that he learned a whole new behavioral pattern and sure learned a new vocabulary. What can I say?

So, time to substitute. It wasn't going to get any better.

Ramier was a freshman and was our sixth man. He was a pretty fair player, although not as good as he thought.

He was a rather free soul, with a ponytail. A flower child wannabe if you please. Nothing wrong with this, just my feeling.

Our relationship from the first weeks of practice was interesting to say the least. He let me know I shouldn't yell at him. He would pretend to ignore me, not looking at me when I did yell at him. But I knew he heard me. If nothing else, I'm loud and for someone not to hear me in a gym, they would have to have a significant hearing loss. I think I was a cultural shock to him. He probably never dreamed in his worse nightmare that such a person as me really existed.

He was all about make love, not war or yellin'n such. Hugging is great. Positive reinforcement.

We clashed, pure and simple.

Since I was in charge, no, make that in control for this particular enterprise; he had to put up with me if he wished to continue to be part of the team. This he did. But his way, not mine.

Ain't going to happen Charlie.

He would tell me he could 'tune me out.'

Again, knowing that I had a great gym voice, loud and distinctive, I would just smile and would go on. Each of us dealing with the situation as best we could.

All during this game I could hear him in behind me on the bench make remarks about how poor certain people were playing and of course how he could do better. I must confess that after watching more of the same out on the floor, I was ready to agree with him.

After I gave him the order to take off his jacket, which meant I was going to put him in I heard him mutter, "Its about time."

My reaction was quick and to the point.

"Ramier, put your jacket back on."

To punctuate the point, I never put him in for the entire game. Just to let him know who was in charge.

It's not nice to mess with Mother Nature—or your coach!!!!

Hong Kong.

It was a wonderful trip for everybody. We had a journalist for our trip to Hong Kong. After we returned home I received the following day-to-day diary. The only problem is I can't remember who composed it. And I'm too embarrassed to ask. It was our Rehabilitation nurse, Maren Larson or Dan Snobl's wife, Mary. To either one I thank very much. Thus:

On December 17, 1985, the Broncos, Southwest State University's wheelchair basketball team began a ten-day odyssey that would see them play wheelchair basketball games in Hong Kong and in the People's Republic of China in Canton.

Three basketball games were played. The first on December 22, the Broncos played the local Hong Kong team at the Jubilee Sports Center. The game was played on an outdoor court. The Broncos won 31–24. Tim Grages with 14 points and Kurt Greniger with 12 led the way. The second game was the following day in Canton, China. After a long, five hour train trip, the Broncos defeated the Canton team 35–24. Kurt Greniger with 12 points and Bob Lamb with 10 were the two top scorers. On the 25th, after a day off, the final game ended in an unusual 39–39 tie against the Hong Kong team, again at Jubilee Sports Center. Bob Lamb made two free throws with three seconds to go to put the game into overtime, but our host opted that these were friendly games and did not wish to play the overtime period. We complied with their wishes and thus for the first time in our history have recorded a tie to our game results. Greniger led the way with 17 points followed by Mike Laven with 10. 1

The idea for the tour came from David Leung, a student at SSU and a member of the Broncos. He discussed the possibilities with Lew Shaver, Coach of The Broncos, prior to returning home for the summer of '85. Through participation as a Bronco, David became aware of the lack of accessibility and activity programs in and around his home environ.

Returning in the fall, David indicated that he had an invitation from the Sports Association for the Physically Handicapped in Hong Kong from Sports Coordinator, Mr. Martin Lam. A proposal was presented to Southwest. After careful review, the President of the University, Dr. Robert Carothers approved the tour and pledged the necessary support.

Parallel to the acquisition of institutional approval, the tour sought and received endorsement from the National Wheelchair Basketball Association, Dr. Stan Labanowich, Commissioner. Dr. Labanowich then assisted SSU in securing sanction from the Amateur Basketball Association United States of America. A proclamation was presented to the Broncos from the Governor of Minnesota, Rudy Perpich, proclaiming Southwest State University Broncos to be honorary representatives of the State of Minnesota.

The group included eleven student-athletes, Head Coach Lew Shaver, Trainer R.A. Colvin, and Medical Staff, Dan Snobl, R.P.T. and Maren Larson, R.N., and Dr. Lynn Cupkie, Dean of Students at SSU, who assumed the duties of the Chief of Mission. Additional family members included Mrs. Mary Snobl, Mrs.

Lou Ann Colvin, Mr. Dennis Larson, Dr. Cupkie's two children, Michelle and Todd, and Lew Shaver's son, Derek.

Student recruitment was a primary consideration. The eleven basketballs players were all student-athletes at SSU. It was stressed throughout the effort that this be utilized in efforts to recruit prospective students.

SSU is one of only a few universities to include wheelchair athletes into the total athletic program. This was incorporated into all presentations and seminars.

Thus, from the initial concept, the tour was viewed in broad terms. A basic program of seminars/workshops was developed. This effort included the medical classification aspects relevant to disabled activities and competition, roles of coaches and administrators within disabled sports programs, and organization and administration of activities in public schools and community. Wheelchair basketball was the primary modality.

The basic theme was to focus on skill-development and the resultant independence disabled individuals can achieve. Fund raising efforts for the tour came from a variety of sources. The primary support was developed through the President's office. A generous donation from the SSU Student Health Services, Dan Snobl, Director, was pledged. Student organizations pledged support. A wheelchair benefit game against community, business individuals and SSU faculty raised a substantial sum. The list is endless and the support and excitement afforded the project was outstanding.

And finally on December 17, the group boarded an American Airlines flight in Minneapolis-St. Paul bound for Los Angeles via Dallas, Texas, then to Anchorage, Alaska, to Seoul, Korea and some thirty-six hours later by Korean Airlines to Hong Kong. Because of the international dateline, we arrived in Hong Kong on the 19th.

Our hosts at both sites were most gracious. In addition to the sports oriented seminars the medical staff was invited to tour the Mac Lehose Medical Rehabilitation Center. We were able to observe, share, and compare each country's efforts directed toward getting people back into society and experience in-dependent living.

Prior to each game, the traditional presentation and exchange of gifts took place between team members. After the first game, our host from Hong Kong gave a reception. Southwest presented the Sports Association a gold plate commemorating the occasion and several copies of an Attendant Manual authored by Mr. Snobl and Mrs. Larson and the Concepts and Techniques of Wheelchair Basketball manual authored by Mr. Shaver.

The Sports Association made available three vans for our use during our stay. We were housed in the Hong Kong Regency that is located in the heart of the downtown area. With the vans and our two, own personal guides, David and his sister, Addie Leung, we spent our time sight-seeing and touring in grand fashion. Hong Kong is a vibrant and exciting environ. Add this fact to the Christmas and holiday season and you have the ingredients for a most unique experience.

Another highlight occurred when David Leung, Kurt Greniger, and Lew Shaver appeared on the T.V. show "Good Morning, Hong Kong" at 7:30 a.m. on the 24th. We departed on the 26th and arrived back home in the Twin Cities area on the 27th, having regained our last day.

To summarize, I think one could say we were exhausted, but deliciously so. The area in and around Hong Kong is not as accessible as here in the States. That, with the train and bus transfers plus the airline changes, offered us many experiences in the art of loading and unloading. Due to the efforts of all involved, there were no major crises, no major personality conflicts, only cooperation and thus our exhaustion was only a small nuisance compared to our lasting memories.

Eating On The Road.

The bus pulled into the team's favorite place—MacDonald. I could hear the mummers from those that were awake, one in particular. "Aw shit, Mac again." But I knew deep down they were thrilled to death, not to mention hungry.

Chinese fire drill number umpteen (that's a lot) is about to begin. Past experience had taught me that on long road trips, stopping at a fast food place was the easiest and quickest. It takes time, sometimes too long, to unload every player, go in for a sit-down meal and then go through the loading process again. This would normally take at least and hour and a half. The idea was to get us back in time for some sleep before some of us had to be at an eight o'clock class the next morning. Every little half-hour helped.

This particular return trip, from the University of Wisconsin, Whitewater was a good nine to ten hours. We had played a game on this Sunday morning and by the time we loaded and were on the road home it was close to two in the afternoon. The math was simple.

I had a friend who always referred to the three or four o'clock in the morning arrivals as 'dark thirty.' The 'dark thirties' were not my favorite arrivals. To lecture at eight the same morning was a struggle. I mean, to be my brilliant self after only a couple of hours sleep was asking a bit. Bright eyed and bushy tailed. I didn't want to join the students who did sleep through some of these. Doesn't look good for the professor to nod.

So the team would eat on Lew Shavers' time schedule—a fast food place. Hey, I'm in charge, right?

I can't really recall all the warm and fuzzy reactions this got over the years. 'Aw shit' was mild. But it would usually go something like this, "Coach, we can't eat another gut bomb." But you know, it's amazing what people will eat when they are hungry. So the 'aw shit' comment was nothing new or troublesome and it sure didn't change the situation.

After a few years, I had the routine down to a science. Practice makes perfect you know.

As we pulled into the parking lot we could see the workers inside and their reaction was always interesting. I could detect panic when they would see the bus. Our bus was an over-the-road coach, capacity of 47 or so. A big honker. We could see the workers scrambling. And the later we were the more scramble we could see.

Even though all the fast food places advertise that buses are welcome it's the employees that have to deal with a gob of people, most of which are demanding immediate service—NOW!!!! Got to be a zoo, not to mention a pain in the ass. Got to give credit where credit is due, most of our visits were met with friendly, smiling and courteous service.

This was particularly late, about a quarter to ten, just before closing time. We still had some three hours to go.

I'm sure the workers were thinking about cleaning up and getting to a hot date of whatever, anything but one more damn, big bus.

Only three or four of us would actually get off the bus and go in to order. I could see the relief and jubilation. But their joy was short lived. We had taken orders on the bus and like Santa, had our list and would check it twice before we pulled in. We were ready as soon as the bus pulled to a stop.

I would approach the counter with the food order in hand. The poor worker was unsuspecting as to about what was to befall them. They would be smiling, waiting. And I would begin:

'ten big Macs'

'eight quarter pounders with cheese'

'four fish'

By now the worker would be stunned. I would start all over again. Same response. Finally, I would assure them that this was for real. No kidding. For a third time:

'ten big Mac'

'eight quarter pounders with cheese'

'four fish'

'six hamburgers'

'six cheeseburgers'

'four chicken mac nuggets'

'assorted sauces, ketchup, and so on

'fourteen small fries'

'ten large cokes'

'four milks'

'two salads'—for the vegetarians, I would add.

Check the list, anything more? Nope. That's all.

By this time the manager had been notified and the true fast food process was about to happen at its finest.

The manager noticing there were only three or four of us would look out at the bus. This guy was no dummy. He finally asked, "This is all to go, right?" I nodded. He continued to look perplexed. I then explained that we were a wheelchair basketball team on out way home to Southwest. No one ever seemed to know where or what Southwest was. And we were in Minnesota. Kinda puts some of all this in perspective. I took a few moments to tell him about dear little old Southwest. He nodded. Didn't say anything, just nodded.

I told him this was the quickest way for us to eat. The mention of a wheelchair basketball team seemed to galvanize the place. "Wow'" would come an exclamation from some worker followed up with something to the effect that I must really be special to coach something like that and what courage it took for 'them' to play and that they had watched the Special Olympics on TV, and how wonderful it all was.

I never had the heart to tell people who would invariably respond with all this bullshit that no, there was not any real courage, that some of 'them' were real pains in the ass, and for goddamn sure I wasn't special, just tired and hungry.

But I would smile and accept the extra promptness and vigor that our order was now receiving while hearing the remarkable occurrence spread throughout the rest of the workers. Again, whatever works.

The mayhem was about to begin. Two or three of the other workers were now helping with the order. Food and drink were coming fast, sacks appeared, and then one of the workers asked, "Is this for here or to go?" The manager hopped right on this and assured her it was to go. Teamwork, you gotta love it.

The thought did cross my mind, "Did anyone really think three or four of us were going to eat all this food in here?"

The system was humming, working in full gear and to perfection. And what a system it was. We were checking the list once again. The student managers were beginning to carry out the sacks.

Now the real fun part. Since we had taken all the orders, in bulk, before we stopped, this meant that everyone would have to remember what they had ordered. But hey, these were college students, no problem. There were no individual orders to be carried out one at a time. Everything was done in bulk. So as a sack was filled, out it went, sort of express line fashion.

Once on the bus we would walk down the aisle yelling, "Who ordered this?' At any one time there could be two or three of us distributing food. So listen up was the order of the moment.

All in all a bit chaotic, but the upper class players would teach the rookies the various ways and means. This includes be nice, courteous, cooperative, and don't whine as this pisses off the coach. The coach would remember this at the next practice.

I would always order a few extra because there would almost certainly be a player who would forget what they had ordered or would decide they wanted something else. Good luck at this point. And, of course, there was invariably the 'vegetarian' who did not like anything and would mumble about stopping at a lousy fast food place. This was greeted with my usual, cheerful demeanor, especially if the weekend had been tough and long. Translation, "If we had got our butts kicked, be nice to the old fart." All these types of comments would go over like the 'lead balloon.'

There was sort of a glitch. The aisle became crowded as the food was being distributed. In addition to the food distributors, there was always someone who had to get off the bus for one reason or another and would return at the same time as the food. If this were a player in a wheelchair, there would be times I or someone would l have to lift and carry them back on board. The aisle would be cleared to the command of, "coming through." The heavier the person, the more critical this became.

On this night, one of the players, a double, above the knee amputee, thought it would be a great deal of fun to 'walk' up and down the aisle using the backs of the seats. As I returned with one of the first sacks he was coming down the aisle towards the front of the bus doing his acrobatic act. His body would pendulum back and forth as he went from one pair of seats to another.

I had to admit it was entertaining as hell and I hated to stop such a performance, but the situation seemed to demand such action. Thought I'd seen it all.

Twenty minutes and the bus was back on the road. It worked well in retrospect. The bus driver had his break and had eaten. In and out. On the road again.

The Blizzard.

Normally, the bus ride back from Wisconsin is about a nine-hour trip. But with a blizzard smacking southwestern Minnesota on a Sunday afternoon, the journey became a real overnighter for us.

After weekend games against other intercollegiate teams at the University of Wisconsin at Whitewater our bus became stranded just about thirty-eight miles south of Marshall, in Slayton, Minnesota.

The bus slid into a snow bank after veering to miss a small truck stranded out in the middle of the highway and became stuck.

There were no injuries, and the biggest complaint was simple boredom, at least for a while. There were snacks, and the warmth of the bus, so no immediate concern.

In all my years we had never been stuck on a bus before. We had several trips that we had to pull in somewhere on the way home, but had been lucky I guess and always made it to a town and usually into a motel.

In defense of the driver, the decision was after some serious discussion as we turned off the interstate and headed north, only seventy miles from home with some hours of daylight remaining. When it comes to push and shove, the driver has the final say, but it was a consensus choice to drive on.

I remember feeling some uncomfortable thoughts. A wheelchair team is different. A number of our players weren't going to just get up and walk off if anything happened. But over the years we had never been stuck and in weather worse than this, so onward.

Just before getting stuck I looked over at my student-assistant, Thomas Williams. He was one of these people that could sleep anywhere. He also seemed to be able to fall asleep in an instant. And snore! Oh my God, he rocked the bus. And he wasn't alone. Harry Jones, a dear friend and teaching colleague for many years, was with us as an official for the weekend and he could also honk'em pretty good. Together they were a major chorus. No one else was asleep, trust me. But, and this is important, they were both big, especially Thomas. I could put up with a little noise.

The cacophony ceased in a hurry when the bus slid into the snow bank. By now the wind was howling, as around fifty miles an hour. And it continued to snow. And snow.

After about an hour it got dark and the mood began to change. I was thinking, hindsight being what it is, that we sure shouldn't have been on the road. Getting stupidity out of the way, a local Sheriff had gotten stuck and was being dug out when someone noticed our headlights. When they investigated, there we were.

A couple of people were suddenly on the bus and letting us know they would send for help. By this time the snow was piled up as high as the windows in the bus. I had my doubts about getting pulled out and already thinking about how to get some of the players off the bus if people could get to us in snowmobiles or whatever. It wasn't time to panic, but if I said I wasn't feeling some real concern, a bolt of lightning might strike me.

I think the kids were calmer than I. No screaming or yelling or outburst.

We were stranded for about three hours before real help arrived. I could see people walking outside the bus—walking by the windows. Maybe stage two-panic.

Eventually, a tractor-powered snow blower reached us followed by a front-end loader. They hooked us up to the front-end loader and the now with the snow blower leading the way, we were pulled out.

We were taken to an Implement Dealer in Slayton to spend the night. Before we knew, people were coming in on snowmobiles bring sandwiches, blankets, coffee, pop, and a portable T.V. I kid you not.

While spending a night in a garage may not seem like paradise, to us it was the next best thing. We spread out, sleeping in the showroom, on the floor, and wherever we could find a place. Me, I slept in the back seat of a showroom car as far away from Harry and Thomas as I could get. We didn't need their lifting. But they slept like they had put in a twelve-hour day in the coalmines. You had to be there.

We were O.K. We were safe.

The spectacle.

Let's see, is there a kind way to say this? No, not really. In all my glory, I was trying to impress my new wife, Judy and most of her family. She had several brothers and sisters in the immediate area plus her parents and they were nearly all at my game.

As I recall it was a Saturday afternoon game. To make it a rather short story, on Monday, the local newspaper reported, "Broncos coach, Lew Shaver, who was called for two technical fouls that the rollers turned into four easy free throws, said he should take part of the blame for the loss." We were playing a team out of Mankato the Key City Rollers, final score 49–45.

I was quoted, "I got nailed twice for technicals and that ought not to happen…there's no excuse. Because of that I feel I certainly played a part in the loss."

Whoa, just a second, I really said, "No excuse?" There is always an excuse, right? The fact that we shot something like seven out of thirty-one field goal attempts the second half, plus twelve turnovers the same half probably had something to do with it.

Add this bit of information to the fact that my two best friends were officiating, R.A. Colvin and Harry Jones, who in a critical part of the game went blind or brain dead or both, and I have a case for lots of excuses. Sure I do!!!

All this happened later in the second half, with about six minutes to go and the score tied or only a one-point game. I had been calm most of the game; at least I thought so. Then in about ten seconds my good buddies missed two traveling violations by the Rollers. Two!!! And these guys are the home team officials. On the first missed call I was up and screamed that they had just missed a traveling, with an added emphasis of Goddammit.

I learned later that Judy's sister, up in the bleachers, leaned over to Judy and whispered something to the effect that shouldn't I be getting a technical?

At about the same time my two myopic zebras missed the second traveling. This was too much and up I came again with a few soft verbalizations questioning their eyesight in a most gentlemanly manner, got my first technical. Not engaging my brain before talking I think I said something to the effect that this was bullshit to which one responded with a warning that if I didn't want another technical to sit down. You can guess what came next. I, my manhood being challenged, dared them to do it. They did!

OOOps, not a good move. Not only did the Rollers get four free throws, which they made; they got the ball and scored. A six-point swing. Not too bright.

So, not only did we lose the game, but also I made a complete ass out of myself in front of all my in-laws. Nice going, way to make points.

Game over, no hard feelings toward my two buddies. And in this I do not kid anyone, myself included. We had a few grins toward each other and a handshake. We were always able to do this.

I could tell when I returned out of the dressing room after handing out towels to the team that the air was tense. Judy's people chatted with me, expressing who they enjoyed watching wheelchair basketball, and some other small tale. They left rather quickly.

It was on the way home that Judy finally let me know she had something to share with me. Oh-oh, I knew I had screwed up. And I was going to hear about it. After telling me she had something to share with me, she sat, quiet for a while. Hated these times all my life. I always knew that what followed wasn't going to be good. She finally said, "Do you know what you were today? You were a, a, a, and then a long pause, a spectacle."

I looked at her in disbelief. She said nothing more. I paused and then said, "Wow, I've been called a lot of things, like an SOB, and so forth, but never a spectacle."

But a spectacle is as a spectacle does.

It wasn't the end of the episode. Later on we had a number of serious talks about why people do some of the things we do. Trust me, a number of discussions.

5

Our World and Welcome To It

First Date.

"How would you like to shit in your pants on the first date?"

I honestly can't say I can imagine something like this happening.

Several of the team was sitting around in one motel room. We had played a game earlier in the evening, returned to our motel and somewhat as usual ordered pizzas and some pop for our post game meal.

I gotta tell you, it is a real thrill to watch growing boys eat, especially college age. Some can really pack it away. This always reminded me of my high school teaching days when I would have lunchroom duty. All I can say is that when I saw the movie, *Animal House*, I could relate!

Sometimes I would reserve a conference room in the motel to gather for this feasting or not finding this as an option, would simply designate one of the players rooms.

Never mine!

We would reserve five or six rooms depending on the number and gender make up of the team.

A rule of thumb I learned rather quickly, in assigning rooms, was not to put more than three players in a double room. The idea was to put a 'walker', a player not requiring a wheelchair in every room. Two wheelchairs in a room was a room full and the 'walker' was for emergency and/or assistive help. We usually left his chair out in the bus, travel trailer or at the gym if we could. Our budget was such that we could not afford only two to a room, but I always thought four was just too many.

This left two beds in a room with three people. I left it up to the players to decide who slept with whom. One player, usually an upperclassman, could have a bed alone while the other two had to 'buddy-up.' On occasion I had to make a decision when personalities conflicted or whatever. I learned that like Virginia, "there is a Santa Claus," that yes, Lew, there are disabled individuals who are a pain in the ass and no one wants to be around them, especially all night. It did not take a brain surgeon to guess, given one player was huge or be a senior and the other a 'rookie' who took the single bed route.

After we ate, we would usually rehash the game we played earlier, win or lose. I would share the game stats and how I felt about the effort and level of play. We would then discuss what we might try to do for the next game, which would probably be in the following morning. I sensed that being late at night and of course just the inspirational tone of my presentation I attempted to keep it short and simple. Sure I did!!

Winning always seemed to make these talks easier, for the players and me. Surprise, surprise.

After the strategy session, the meeting would turn to general talk better known as a bullshit session.

Then the issue would soon surface—SEX. I can forthrightly and honestly say to one and all that any doubts or misgivings about interest in dating, conquest or failures, interest and such associated with sex and the disabled on my part or awareness were quickly dispelled.

During these sessions I got to hear and was privy to many a hunt or quest, from both the male and female point of view, but mostly from the male side of the situation.

I quickly learned that disability is no indicator or hindrance. There is a definite interest.

As one player put it, "Yeah coach, we're just red blooded American boys."

Over the years this has been reinforced and I have no reason to doubt this.

I'm also aware that male bonding is interesting. It's also predictable. I've heard many females express, "That the male brains are a bit or maybe a lot located between our legs." And, paralysis is no deference.

A physical impairment does not seem to lessen the urge or the verbal diarrhea on the subject. I cannot speak to the female issue with much authority, but I do know that the testosterone flows freely.

As I listened to some of the stories this particular session I was struck by the similarity between my past such experiences. Each story seemed to outdo the previous one, the success ratio measured by the perceived beauty of the fortunate female. Fortunate that is, according to the particular male telling the story. SOS—same old stuff!

This session took a turn that was somewhat unique as the talk shifted to some of the problems and utter failures or embarrassing moments.

The pronouncement of an accident stopped all.

"I'm serious, I shit in my pants." It was good old John Schatzlein.

"Yeah, bullshit," someone muttered.

"True story, I swear."

I think he was suggesting that some of the stories that were being told were a bit exaggerated—just a bit untrue, naw, down right lies!

The floor was his.

"I met my wife, Helen, in a class we were taking, She was an AB, but damn good looking and built. It took me several days before I got up enough courage to ask her out on a date. I explained I was independent, had hand controls on my care and could transfer in and out of my wheelchair. I think she thought I was nuts. I'm not sure she was ready for any of this, but maybe didn't know how to say no to me, which was OK with me. I mean, hey whatever works. I'll be the token gimp."

Several guys sorta laughed at this reference to a 'token gimp'. Affirmative action at the very best—a date.

He continued. "We both lived in the dorms, so on Friday night I met her down in the lounge area. She lived up on the third floor, which was not accessible. So we met in the lower, first floor lounge.

"Yeah," someone pipped up, "can't get to all that stuff on the upper floors, what a bitch."

A round of laughter and nodding in agreement plus some additional, rather silly comments followed much of which either went over my head or I couldn't quite hear.

After a few moments, John broke in with, "Anyway, I took her to the show and that is always an interesting experience. The theater people are never sure what to do with the chair or me. I finally convinced them to let me sit on an outside aisle seat next to Helen. I could then fold up my chair and lock it down so I could have it next to me in the aisle. It didn't take long before the manager came down and told me it was against the fire code or some such bullshit to leave anything in the aisle. I asked him if fried cripple would look good in the newspapers if I couldn't get to my chair in case of fire. It was great. He didn't know what to say. We compromised. I folded up my chair and pulled it into the row between the seats. But as I did I got in one more shot asking the manager why there was no handicapped seating. He didn't answer. Pissed me off, no wheelchair seating."

"Ain't that the shittin truth," someone blurted.

"But being the nice guy I am, not to mention trying to empress Helen, I made it work."

This brought silence, until another voice said, "Yeah, right, and friggin cows fly."

I couldn't wait any longer and broke in, "OK, so you're a nice guy, what about the pants bit?"

"I'm getting to that," he said. "We went to *The Chalet* for a late dinner. I, of course, had to go through the kitchen area to get to the dining room. People in chairs get to see all the scenic routes with the greatest olfactory delights, such as garbage dumps by the service entrance."

"John, you're so full of shit," came a voice from across the room.

"Well, dammit, it's the truth. Just like the damn waiter who offered to cut up my steak for me. You guys know, all the bullshit AB's lay on us. But it was good food and all in all a great evening."

"Damn this is a long story," I heard someone say.

"Almost over. I was really feeling good. I think Helen really enjoyed it and as I pulled into the university parking lot I was pretty excited. Too excited. I felt, and trust me, even as a high para, I felt my bowels loosen."

There was a pause with some chuckling, others laughing, some bored.

"And finally'" he said, "The smell was overpowering, so I couldn't fake it. I just looked at her and as calmly as I could told her I had just shit in my pants. She laughed. I swear, she laughed. It was OK. She was great! I knew right then I wanted to marry her."

No one seemed to want to top this bit of history. There was a rather awkward silence. I suggested we turn in as we had a late morning ball game to play and it was eleven o'clock.

There were some diehards still trying to tell a few more tales as most of us left the room saying our good nights.

One Tough Time.

Danny Guetter died in a motorcycle accident two weeks before graduation in the spring of '72. Danny was riding a motorcycle, even though he was single leg, above the knee amputee, down the main street of Marshall when a car making a left hand turn pulled right in front of him. It was about five in the afternoon.

The driver of the car said he never saw him and Danny had no time to turn and broad sided the car, catapulting him into and over the car.

I happened to be in the Rehabilitation Office when the call came through from the police. They were looking for the next of kin to notify them about the accident. They didn't know much about the accident they said and as far as they knew Danny was alive, but they had no word on his condition.

As the secretary kept talking to the police giving them the information they wanted, I sprinted out to my car and raced to the hospital. I found the emergency room, but was informed that there was no news. After a few moments a nurse came out and told me they were rushing Danny up to surgery. He was critical with internal bleeding.

I was standing there when they wheeled him out. He was conscious and actually reached out and brushed my hand as he went by. That's the last time I saw him alive.

The internal damage was too massive. I'm not sure of this sequence, but he either died during the operation or soon after.

His parents joined me after a bit along with other family. I can't remember the time they told us he was dead, must have been nine or ten that evening.

The entire wheelchair team attended the funeral. Danny was from Wabasso, a small farming community about thirty miles southeast of Marshall. It was on the farm he lost his leg. I understood he caught it in an auger and as he told it, "It chewed his leg half-way up his thigh."

His family was great. They never sued the man driving the car. I heard Mr. Guetter tell someone that accidents happen and nothing would bring Danny back. Not many people with that kind of forgiving attitude in this day and age.

As the team and I pulled up across the street from the church in several cars, I heard a voice in the back of my car mutter, "O'boy a Catholic Church, steps."

As I got out of my car, with my wife, there were already several very big guys coming out of the church and down the steps towards us. They had been waiting and looking for us. There must have been twenty or so. Without much fanfare, with some direction from the wheelchair players and myself as to who belonged to what chair, the team was transferred and carried up the steps and into the church. His parents met my wife and I at the door and escorted us towards the front of the church where an area had been reserved for the team.

We were taken out to the cemetery and to the funeral meal at the Guetter farm and each time, help was provided. There was no way the team was going to be excluded from this occasion. It seemed like the whole town of Wabbasso was involved. Wonderful people.

Tough day, but certainly a loving one.

One of a Kind.

In the fall of '76 I got a letter and a flyer from Larry Foukas. Larry had attended Southwest for a couple of years, played a little wheelchair basketball and generally lit up my life. He was one of the truly funny people I have ever known. He had a quick mind and a great way of saying things. Can't explain it any more than this, just a funny guy.

He was a double amputee, both above the knees. One leg amputation was all the way up, including the hip while the other side had a very short stump. He was a big guy, filling up a wheelchair except the whole front end would be empty. He had transferred to Mankato State sometime after '73 or '74 to finish a degree in counseling. I hadn't heard from him since, so I was surprised to receive the packet.

The flyer was a stitch. I'll try to describe it. It was titled TRIPPIN' 'n' WHEE-LIN.' This was printed up at the top of a single page. He evidently had had done it free hand. It was big, ballooned printing; very bold and very black. He had drawn what appeared to be a wheelchair moving with a puff of wind in back of it. In the upper, right hand corner was partly typed and printed, *Another Sterling Presentation From the Presses of Office of Handicapped Services.*

Below all this was a double parallel line about three spaces wide with the date, July, 1976 on the left, Happy birthday America in the middle, and Holy Moly, Still Free on the right side of the paper.

Underneath this bit of art—cough, cough—was his message. I must confess I used this material in my teaching for a good many years. I thought it said a great deal. I reproduced it for my classes and never asked Larry for his permission. So sue me. His message was:

When You Meet a Handicapped Person

During the course of presenting our awareness sessions we give several hand-outs to the participants. The one that we get the most response from has the above title. I would like to reprint it for you, and I must offer my apologies to the original source because I do not remember where it came from.

1. First of all, remember that handicapped people are people. They are like anyone else except for the special limitations of their individual disabilities.

2. A disability need not be ignored or denied between friends. But until your relationship is that, show friendly interest in them as people.

3. Be yourself when you meet them.

4. Talk about the same things as you would with anyone else.

5. Help them only when they request it. When handicapped people fall they may wish to get up by themselves, just as many blind people prefer to get along without assistance. So offer help but wait for their request before giving it.

6. Be patient. Let the disabled set their own pace in walking or talking.

7. Don't be afraid to laugh with them.

8. Handicapped people deserve the same courtesy, as anyone would receive. Don't stop and stare at the disabled person.

9. Don't be over-protective or over-solicitous. Don't shower handicapped people with kindness.

10. Don't offer pity or charity. Handicapped people want to be treated as equals. They want a chance to prove themselves.

11. Don't separate disabled people from their wheelchairs or crutches unless they request it. They may want them in reach.

12. When dinning with handicapped people, don't offer to help in cutting their food—they will ask you or the waiter if they need help.

13. Don't make up your mind ahead of time about handicapped people. You may be surprised at how wrong you are in judging their interests and abilities.

14. Enjoy your friendship with handicapped people. Their philosophy and good humor will give you inspiration.

This from a person who, along with another player, on the way back from a trip to Des Moines tried to sneeze nearly all the way back without blinking. I made the mistake during some inane conversation that I had read where a person could not sneeze without blinking. These two geniuses stuffed things up their noses, stared at the sun, anything to make them sneeze to prove it was possible. I couldn't believe all the snot they produced. I know, I didn't have to watch, but it was a boring day.

His message produced some interesting discussions over the years.

You're Carrying a What?

The official hand blown his whistle, stopping play.

I just thought that the other team had called a time out and was thinking about what I wanted to say during the time out.

My players were coming off the floor. The official came over to the sideline in-between the two benches and held up an object and asking, "Whose is this?"

Evidently something had fallen on the floor, which wasn't all that unusual. Parts of wheelchairs often came off. Over the year's leg bags would sometimes break, spilling urine all over the floor. All anyone had to do was follow the trail to find the culprit. And then find someone brave enough to wipe or mop it up. I always had a few extra towels in reserve for this duty.

I couldn't see the object but heard one of my players answer. "It's mine," he said as he pushed over and retrieved the object. I noticed a quizzical look on the officials face as he handed it over to him.

As the kid pushed back to our huddle I looked at the player and asked, "What is it?" And then I saw it, a knife. Not just a pocketknife, but a rather long one. "What the hell are you doing with that?" I demanded.

"To protect myself," he answered.

"In a damn basketball game?" I shot back at him.

"Never know," he shrugged.

I took the knife from him. I think for a split second he was thinking about not giving it up. My 'if you don't give it up, you're dead look' convinced him to fork it over.

He mumbled something as he started back out on the floor. That was too much; didn't hear what he said but I was damn sure it wasn't complimentary.

I stopped him in his tracks and took him out of the game, where he sat for most of the rest of the game.

After the game I gave it back to him and asked him where in the hell did he keep it during the game? He showed me that he was wearing a three-quarter-boot type shoe and would slip it in the side of the shoe. I just shook my head and rolled my eyes. I also informed him that should I find out he continued this wonderful little paranoid bit of behavior; he would be in deep shit.

I found out I wasn't the only coach to experience something like this. I shared this story with a dear fiend from New Jersey, Al Youakim, who has been in wheelchair basketball for time before dirt, for fifty years and more. One of the true pioneers of the sport. He laughed and informed me that in his experience with a community team out of New Jersey, they found all kinds of legal and illegal crap, including a gun. He could tell I thought he was bullshitting me and crossed his heart and held up his right hand proclaiming, "I shit you not, we had a guy who dropped a gun on the floor during a game."

God I was glad to coach college kids.

He's No Quad.

Unbelievable I thought as I read the newspaper article.

In the span of some six weeks or so, two young teen-age boys in a small community had been severely injured resulting in quadriplegic. Two in a small area. Just unreal. What are the percentages of this happening? A million to one? Two, three or more million to one?

These accidents had happened over the summer and each boy had gone through about a year of intensive therapy.

Both were beginning to return to the community to continue their life. They were attending classes at the local high school.

The article followed each boy through his accidents, one farm related, the other a car accident. It chronicled how each family was attempting to adjust and how the community was responding with support such as fundraisers.

As I read I was detached from the emotionalism of the article. I had been working with any number of quadriplegics in the wheelchair sports program. This provided me with a bit of objectivity. I realized I could afford to be objective, to be detached as it were. I wasn't directly involved. Neither of these kids were one of my own.

I wondered, with each article I read, what my feelings and reaction would be if it were one of mine.

Much different, I'm sure. A father once told me that it is impossible to explain the pain and anguish. There are no words.

I often felt that my reaction and many others like me would be like coming upon a nasty accident where there are clearly injured people. I notice, when this occurs, that as I drive by slowly, my thoughts are something to the effect about how horrible this situation is and a sense of sorrow and pity for the injured. But for the Grace of God go I.

The effect on me seems to last a few miles, maybe more. I actually reduce my speed after I pass the scene. Then, perhaps ten miles of so, guess what—I'm back up to my original, speed and my life goes on.

I've noticed myself thanking God it wasn't me. Sometimes I tell Him I will be a better person as if He can be bargained with or influenced by my spiritual announcement.

In any case, as coincidence would have it, a few weeks later I received a phone call from the Superintendent of the school district the boys were attending. He inquired about the possibility of a community event at the high school and our wheelchair basketball team being a part of the fund raising efforts.

His idea was to feature our wheelchair students in an intra-squad game with perhaps a demonstration of wheelchair mobility. He had heard about the Southwest program threw an Occupational Therapists who serviced his school district working with several disabled students, now including these two boys.

The Superintendent informed me, that both young men were rather high quadriplegics. He said this was his impression. I asked about their use of a manual wheelchair and he told me he thought they were both using electric models.

We chatted about some other, general issues before I assured him we could agree on a date and time. I also indicated that we would or could bring our Physical Therapist for additional functional evaluation. He agreed to this immediately and thanked my for the thought. Any expertise or experience would be welcome.

It was agreed that we would be reimburse for our travel expenses and that the district would host a meal in the school cafeteria. I suggested that the two boys and their families be invited to the meal.

The Superintendent asked about how to advertise the evening and what I thought the cost to the public ought to be. I gave him several options, but basically told him he knew his community better than I. We would send press releases over if this would help. He also asked if I would consent to being interviewed by the local radio station. Being the ham I am, that was easy—of course.

All was set.

Four weeks hence we readied our caravan to go over. I made arrangement to arrive early with Mike Haig, one of our disabled students, specifically a quadriplegic. In my experience, in these situations, it is much more effective to have a person with a similar disability work with the families. Something about peer counseling that is effective.

I attempted to be aware, even in my most egocentric moments, either in working with an individual or groups of people who were disabled, I would walk away from such encounters. What a difference. For me to think my words would work miracles was an illusion and not the least bit of arrogance. And as some mortals are prone, I had my share of arrogance.

Mike was a senior business major, an honor student who was already accepted into Law School after graduation. He had participated in our wheelchair track and field program with success, qualifying for the national games in several events. He was also a member of the wheelchair basketball team.

In addition, and I personally felt this was important, he used a manual wheelchair and was very independent.

On the afternoon of the game, I made arrangements for the team to load and come at a later time.

Mike and I left some two hours early.

The two kids and their families were waiting for us outside the school on a loading dock and ramp. I could see the group even before we were at the school. An individual who seemed to have some authority or maybe just a busybody directed me to a parking area. I was directed to a parking space that had a sign indicating it was reserved for service vehicles. It had direct access to the ramp that led up to the loading dock.

As I got out of the car, the gentlemen who had directed me where to park quickly identified him self as Superintendent So-and-so. I shook his hand, introducing myself and gesturing to Mike introduced him.

I got Mikes' wheelchair from the trunk of the car, opened it and placed it where Mike could transfer. I then left him to complete the transfer. I knew he had the skill and did not need my help. In a normal situation, Mike would transfer into his own car and pull his wheelchair in behind him into the backseat area. This is not always the case with quadriplegics, but I knew Mike well.

The boys and their families were fixated on Mikes' progress. There was a real look of disbelief. They were shaking their heads and talking in low tones as I walked up the ramp to meet them. They were so engrossed with Mike that they barely acknowledged my presence and introduction. Each person just sorta nodded to me as I went around the group.

It took Mike a couple of minutes to complete the transfer, find the curb cut, and push up the ramp onto the dock area. I introduced Mike to the two boys and allowed the rest of the entourage to introduce themselves. I'm terrible with names, so took the easy way out.

We stood outside for a bit with nothing but chitchat. I could hear Mike and the boys sharing their accidents and some items about their rehab experience. Small talk.

We were invited to go into the building by good old' Superintendent So-and-so. As we turned to go inside, one of the mothers turned to her son and in a soft voice that I could hear say, "He ain't no quad."

Mike and the two families were in for an interesting evening.

I just smiled to myself and kept walking.

I heard one of the boys ask Mike, "What level are you?"

Leave the real expert alone.

Talk About Ugly.

How ugly can it get? Pretty damn ugly and mean looking and life threatening! Bedsores, pressure sores, decubitus. Like a rose is a rose is a rose, and by any other name still a rose, a pressure sore is a pressure sore, by any other name.

And I was staring at a dandy. "Oh, Jesus Porter, what the hell were you thinking?" I said as I looked at him lying on his side with a naked lamp bulb rather close to his butt.

"Did you see the school nurse before we left?" I asked or actually growled.

"She said I could come if I took care of myself," he offered.

"Yeah, right, and pigs fly," I responded.

"Honest coach I did."

God it was an ugly. I said that before, right? The sore was an open wound about two or three inches across and deep up underneath one side of his butt. "I'm trying to keep it dried out," he said, "and I've got antibiotics."

"Wonderful, I'll put that on your tombstone. He had antibiotics."

"You needed me coach."

"Not at the risk of your life ding-dong! What's your temperature?"

"About 102 or so."

"O.K., we've already played one game and obviously you're here. We've got two hours before game time this morning. We need to make sure everything is clean and padded as much as we can. I'm not sure what the hell to do with this. So I'm going to trust you to do what is right. O.K.?"

Another player volunteered to help him. I remember looking at him and shaking my head yes, but not saying a word.

The other player assured me he knew what he was doing, having had several sores over the years. We were in Des Moines, it was a Sunday and we would return to Marshall by bus in the afternoon. After weighing the pros and cons, I said, "It's a go, but for God's sake fellows, let's make sure we do this right."

With some real misgivings, I did play Porter in the morning game. We nursed him home on the bus.

He saw the nurse Monday morning. She immediately got him off his butt for a good week or so. She also questioned my decision to play him. I'm being kind to myself. She actually told me in no uncertain terms I had opened myself up to some serious problems, not the least would be legal action if something terribly wrong would have happened, like him developing a life threatening infection.

My only thought was, "God does take care of dumb animals…and coaches."

The Yellow River.

The kid at the pump just stood there, acting as though nothing was going on. We had stopped at a small town gas station during one of our long road trips. I always made the excuse that I either needed gas or that one of the players had to empty a leg bag. Any excuse I could think would be appropriate. The truth of the situation is I have, what the kids called TB or tiny bladder. I can blame genetics as my father is blessed with the same condition. He or I don't pass many rest areas on the interstate.

So I had stopped, went potty and topped off the gas tank. The attendant was a rather tall 'drink of water,' skinny and young. He came out of the station office, informing me that this was a full service station and he would pump the gas.

We were traveling in two state station wagons with mine pulling a trailer which was loaded to the gills with all our paraphernalia.

The attendant assured one of my players, a para in a wheelchair, that the rest room was accessible. The rest room was around the corner of the station. The key had to be secured from the attendant. I noticed the quizzical look he gave as he gave the key to the player.

Several chairs were unloaded and a shuttle system was established to allow those that need to transfer to 'relieve' themselves. The first player returned, shaking his head and mumbling about the stupid restroom.

After hearing these mutterings I walked around to the restroom to check out the situation. I walked back to the attendant and explained to him that there was a step up into the restroom and that even if this was overcome; the doorway was too narrow for a wheelchair.

I got a quizzical look and a shrug. The kid didn't have a clue. In the meantime I noticed a few of our players were caucusing. I wasn't privy to their conversation, but was most definitely privy to their decision and action.

The players had noticed the station wagons swear parked on an incline in such a way that should they empty their leg bags behind the trailer, of sight of the attendant, that the urine would run down in front of the pumps, where guess who was standing, filling the tanks.

Imagination aside, here was this yellow river running where this kid was standing. Urine has its own, pungent smell—in other words, it stinks!! And urine collected in a leg bag for several hours reaches a level of fermentation that is not to be ignored!

The attendant stood in this flowing stream of liquid acting as if nothing was happening. He finished filling both station wagons and not once even hinted anything was different. But the smell was almost overpowering to the point of gagging me.

And the wheelchair crew?

They had a good laugh. Accessible their butts.

I just shook my head, paid the bill and was on our way.

Revenge is interesting.

Ode to a C.P.

I could always hear him coming three halls away toward the physical therapy area.

My office was across the hall from the PT area, so I was privy to all the minute-to-minute comings and goings.

He would usually stick his head in my doorway and invariably I would hear, "Hi Lew, I'm back."

He was Pete Martin, a young student who due to a birthing accident was cerebral palsied. He could walk with the aids of 'sticks' but would drag a foot.

Thus I would hear his two 'sticks' hit the floor and hear as he would drag that one foot before swinging his sticks' forward again, creating a familiar rhythm with a sort of click, scrape, click, scrape pattern which would announce him coming where ever he would go. This was magnified and echoed up and down the halls.

We had become good friends. He tried to play wheelchair basketball but found the limitations due the cerebral palsy were too much to overcome for him to participate at the varsity level. We worked for some time but in the end he came to me with his decision not to continue. I encouraged him, as an option, to continue to practice and enjoy what he found he could do. His decision was to concentrate on his studies and physical therapy requirements

This was one of my first experiences with this situation and I wanted so bad to include him, perhaps out of pity and sympathy. I suggested all kinds of modifications and adaptations and some rather unique and not too appropriate I suspect.

He let me know it was OK for him not to be able to play. He reminded me that everyone has limitations and he appreciated the opportunity to find out about his capabilities. The reality of the situation he told me was that the game of wheelchair basketball with its demands was beyond him. He was adamant and announced that he, "Did not want nor need some damn AB playing with his mind."

He reminded me about our earlier efforts to teach him how to drive. Pete and I had worked hard for at least two summers attempting to teach him to drive. To say he worked hard would not do him justice.

We came to realize that in a parking lot with lots of room and no distractions he could do rather well but once we moved out on the street—it became…interesting. Interesting as in driving on the wrong side of the street.

We had his vision checked, but this did not indicate any particular problem. We vowed to keep trying.

Between Pete and Dan Snobl, our Physical Therapist I learned a ton! I learned to talk less as we drove because this added to Pete's motor distractions. This impaired his focus. In other words, I learned to shut up so he could concentrate.

I learned to encourage him to keep in a flexed position, close to the steering wheel. Any time he extended his arms, it seemed his head and feet would also extend and he would wind up 'stiff as a board' as he would say thus losing significant control of the car. We both agreed this was not conducive to good driving. Dan told me he would explain this to me sometime. Never did.

The end came one afternoon when we got courageous and ventured out on the highway and drove some five miles north of the university. Pete really began to struggle. We stopped and he indicated that after all our hard work, he had had it. "It was not in the cards," he said. "We had given it our best shot," according to him.

Being rather close to home, he ask if he could drive back for 'old times sake.'

I figured, why not, we were in a driver education car—duel controls and all.

As we neared the university a highway patrol car met us. I saw Pete tensing up, his eyes getting as big as saucers and I heard him mutter, "Oh shit!"

And with the, "Oh shit," as he stared at the on coming vehicle, his head turning in the direction taking his shoulders with it—along with the steering wheel.

I swear, this is what happened, almost in slow motion.

I grabbed the wheel just as we were about to cross the centerline and we careened back into our lane. No big deal I thought, not that close.

The state trooper evidently didn't agree. In the rearview mirror I saw his tail-lights light up and his lights go on as he slammed on his brakes, made a quick U-turn and with lights flashing and siren blasting came after us.

I heard Pete mutter, "Oh shit," again. I helped him ease off the road onto the shoulder; put on our emergency lights and waited. I remember thinking, "Oh shit just about sums it up."

As the trooper pulled up behind us I made an instinctive decision. I jumped out of our car and walked back to the patrol car.

I think I startled the trooper. Thinking back, he probably thought I was some junkies buddy or some such thing, thinking he was going to have to defend himself.

I began talking—fast, trying to explain the situation. He had the most incredulous look on his face as if saying, "Now I've heard it all."

He eventually walked over to our car and questioned Pete, making me stay back at the patrol car. He returned shaking his head, told me to drive back to the university. He followed us back all the way.

It was Pete's last lesson with me.

Pete thanked me for my effort and for my honesty, treating him as a person and an athlete. He stated, in no uncertain words he detested it when people treated him like a child, or a china doll, very fragile, something to protect.

As he put it, "I do not need your protection, I don't need you to take care of me. That is my responsibility."

I think, at the end of this visit I said something profound like, "OK, whatever you say Pete."

Pretty good basis for a friendship.

So, there he would be, often standing in my doorway.

One particular day I met him in the hall and for some reason looked down at his feet. I said, "Pete, you've got your shoes on the wrong foot, you 'yo-yo'."

"O'like hell I do," he snapped as he lowered his eyes downward and then muttered, "Well I'll be damn, I really do."

This became a private joke between us and I would remind him every chance I found that kinetic intelligence was a part of his life, in other words, the brain shuts down when the body goes in motion.

He would snicker at this and attribute all of this to CP. He would inform me it was his inherited birthright to make these kinds of mistakes.

He shared with me about his life, whether I wanted to hear it or not. He talked about what it was like to be 'CP', how sometimes other children and adults would not be allowed to play with him because they 'might catch CP.'

There were teachers he informed me that because of his slow speech would treat him as though he was mentally retarded. There were people who would shout at him during conversations, as they seemed to believe he must also be deaf in addition to the obvious physical problems. He would unload and almost always would punctuate his stories with being 'pissed off.'

He would then laugh and remind me that he learned it was better to be 'pissed off' than 'pissed on.'

His favorite story centered on his attempt to enroll in college. His rehabilitation counselor, which he was assigned to and needed, of course, due his handicap, suggested he think about something other than college. Pete would relate this in a very sarcastic tone of voice. And just as sarcastic, he related that this confused him, as his high school career was normal, whatever that meant.

The counselor, who was supposed to be an expert or at least educated about vocational career options would always remind Pete that even though he made it through high school, he was CP. Hell, Pete would reply, he knew that but what did this have to with him going to college. He told me he finally figured it out. After about dozen similar episodes, it dawned on him that the counselor was suggesting high school had been a gift and graduation due to social promotion.

In addition, and this was said with a snarl, CP was being equated to some degree with mental retardation.

After relating this story to me, he leaned back and simply said, "Dumb son-of-a-bitch."

When Pete graduated from Southwest, he willed me his shoes, one minus the entire front toe area. As he put it, "As an indication of his deep respect and friendship for me."

On top of the ugliness of them, God they smelled. I asked him if they had really killed the cow. "Ho-ho, very funny Lew," he relied.

I put the shoes in a sack and left them in my office for a couple of weeks. Then just before graduation I had an inspiration. Anyway, I had a thought. I thought it was inspirational.

I cut the shoes in half, sideways, keeping the toe areas. I glued these front sections side-by-side on a plaque much like you would mount a fish. I took the plaque to a jeweler and had engraved on a plate below the fish, oops, I mean the toes, "Ode to a CP."

Hey, I'm no small timer; nothing is too good for my friends. I presented the plaque to him at the annual rehabilitation banquet with all the proper dignity the occasion demanded.

To this day, Pete says the plaque is one of his truly treasured possessions.

Sure it is!!

Pretend A Gimp.

"Ain't he something else? Hell coach, he walks better than you," said Rick.

He was Randy. He was coming down the hall pushing his game chair as he walked in behind it.

And Rick was right. He did walk rather well. As a matter of fact I could not see any limp or gait pattern problem. But our Physical Therapist could and did. Good old Dan Snobl, the PT and I were walking down a hall earlier in the year on our way to the Student Union for a cup of coffee. Dan was one of the great supporters of the wheelchair sports program and was always looking for players for us.

He and I kidded each other that we were a couple of the few people that when we saw a limp, our eyes would light up.

I recall one young person in a shopping mall up in Minneapolis that I spotted with a limp. He looked at me with an incredible look as I walked up to him and asked if the limp were permanent.

Only one way to find out. Right?

I told him who and what I was. He relaxed a bit, informed me the limp was a football injury and would heal.

I thanked him and went on my merry way.

Funny thing though, I got the impression he couldn't wait to get away from me.

Must have been my imagination.

So, much like radar, Dan and I would lock in on anything out of the ordinary walking pattern.

I hadn't spotted Randy down the hall and before we could accost, I mean approach, him he disappeared on us.

Dan kept saying, "Did you see him, did you see him?"

And I kept telling him, "no."

We sounded la bit like Abbott and Costello.

As we entered the Union, Dan assured me he knew the student and would track him down. Thank God for very professional people. In about a week he connected with Randy and encouraged him to see me.

Dan assured me Randy was eligible to play wheelchair basketball, due to a condition in both knees known as chondromalacia. This is characterized by an abnormal softening of cartilage tissue, or something like that.

When Randy came to see me, he told me that he could not play sports in high school because of the pain associated with the condition. He had also been informed that both knees would probably need extensive surgery and perhaps replacement at some time in the future.

As Randy passed by Rick and me, Rick was looking up at me and in a loud voice was suggesting that I, as the coach, should make Randy at least limp to make him look legitimate.

Rick was a para and he and Randy were great friends, so this was being done with a good deal of 'tongue in cheek'.

The verbal bantering went on as Randy continued down the hall on his way to practice, still pushing his chair in front of him.

"Damn pretend-a-gimp," Rick said and smiled.

A little later in an interview for an article about various activities for the International Year of the Disabled, Rick was quoted as saying, "When you're in a wheelchair, it blinks, It's a flashing light that tells everyone you've got a handicap." I felt like this is one of the most profound statements I have ever heard on the disabled. I asked him if it was original, but he just smiled and shrugged. I have a feeling it was.

I kidded him about being a locker room philosopher as later on he was also quoted as saying, "What we're talking about is not that big a deal. What we, the disabled are aiming at is becoming independent. We're hoping they'll (able-bodied population) gain a little etiquette."

With this in mind, plus the close personal friendship that developed between Rick and I, I waited for his reaction to, 'what it meant to be a Bronco' with some anticipation and not just a little curiosity. He wrote:

On July 22, 1976 I had a spinal cord injury. I was 16 at the time. It occurred between my junior and senior year in high school. Things that stick out in my mind is a lot of confusion, a lot of unknowns, a lot of uncertainty as to what the future would hold. As I look back, my knowledge base was directly linked to people that were able-bodied and all I had was a disability and there was a lot of confusion that went with that.

Before I became injured I was involved with football and track at high school and I enjoyed those activities and that is pretty much where my friends came from, those people that enjoyed those activities also.

There are many lessons that are acquired through team sports. Able-bodied people have many opportunities in many different arenas. Disabled people are limited by the opportunities that are available.

Having had the opportunity to participate on a structured team and have had the opportunity to follow the teams' rules and regs, I am now more capable to manage my own personal life and professional aspirations.

By being part of the Bronco team, I have developed a very strong appreciation for what that stands for. There is a certain amount of dignity and pride that come from being able to say that "Yes, I went to SSU and was a part of the Bronco program." this carries over into other aspects of my life. I now have much more confidence in myself by knowing if I try and I stay with it, my goals will become reality. I also know that I have people who support me in these efforts.

The Broncos were critical for me getting through the college curriculum. I had the network of people already in place when I arrived on campus. It was my responsibility to seek these resources out. Our team was on a mission of sorts, the best possible light on and off the court. The decisions we made as a team reflected on our school and more importantly it made a statement of what we were as individuals. These lessons will stay with me for a lifetime.

An example of this pattern is occurring now, years after graduation. I'm involved with organizing a fundraiser for wheelchair sports in our area using my employer, a large cooperation as the catalyst. As part of the evening we have developed a large intra-organizational teams in the cooperation to play a wheelchair basketball tournament.

What is important and the thing that sticks out in my mind goes directly back to what we are doing. I feel that we are on the verge of taking the next step. What I mean by all this is that what we were anticipating in the Rolling Gopher night is that we had employees out, involved, and sitting in wheelchairs. That means we have developed a package. We have something in place and now we are getting other people involved that don't necessarily have disabilities. It makes sense. What you have are people that are able-bodied coming over to Courage Center and getting involved. What that means for me—very personally—is back at work. When I am going through the halls, we can talk wheelchair basketball. They have played wheelchair basketball. They understand that they can see what that means. That is really an enlightening experience.

Another situation is with golf. Able-bodied people volunteer and are able to share an activity together. Granted, they are not playing in chairs, and we are not playing standing up, but the vehicle that we are using is sports. That is our arena. That's what draws us together. It's amazing what I have learned through sports and how that's gotten me exposed to different folks. I have learned through their experiences and through their expertise. Here we are again learning through sports. In my mind, I think that sports overall is the universal language that everyone understands and it is a real strong vehicle to work with other people and to have them take a step in and touch base a little bit and this makes a lot of difference.

It's What Any Normal Person Would Do.

"Well I guess I'm a whole women, huh coach?"

I was at a wedding of one of my former ballplayers, sitting, eating a piece of wedding cake with some punch when this young lady pushed up to me.

"I'd like to introduce my two sons," she said.

The boys, about two and four clung to moms' wheelchair as she introduced them to me. I was thinking they probably were frightened of this 'old fart' in front of them and they both seemed to meld into the wheelchair.

I put on my best smile and they warmed a bit as mom told them I was her basketball coach and I was really a nice man. Moms like to lie like this sometimes to protect their unsuspecting progenies.

I gave each one a high five. They liked that.

Their mother was reminding me of a moment in time when she and I were in the physical therapy room and the occasion that had triggered her remark about being a 'whole' woman.

I was piddling with something when she pushed into the room with a newspaper in her lap and seeing me had exclaimed," Isch coach, just listen to this. Have you read this?"

She handed me the newspaper. Patty was a beautiful young lady from a small town in South Dakota. In her senior year of high school she had won a local beauty contest. "Miss so-and-so,' she would tell people. On the way to a dress fitting for the State contest she was involved in a car accident that left her a high paraplegic.

After her rehabilitation, she found her way to Southwest and became a member of the wheelchair basketball team. She was a delightful, vibrant person, a really upbeat attitude, bright, and had the college guys swarming around her like bees to honey.

She pointed to the article in the newspaper. It was about another young lady in a similar situation who was vowing she would not get married until she, "could walk down the aisle," The article told her story, how she was about to be married, found herself in a situation where life was good. She was about to marry the guy of her dreams.

Then came her accident, on her way to a wedding gown fitting that resulted in her paralysis.

The account related her determination and courage she showed as she went through rehabilitation. And the last paragraph, which indicated the wedding, was off until she could be a whole women and walk down the aisle, she would not think of marriage. She continued explaining she did not think it was fair to the young man involved.

As I finished the article and handed the paper back to Patty, I muttered, "Wow."

"Isn't that a crock of crap," she exclaimed.

"Why?" I responded, "I'm not sure I understand."

"Coach," Patty continued, "she is saying the ability to walk makes her a whole women."

She paused, letting this sink in into my rather obvious bewilderment. Maybe it was the dumb look I gave her that gave her a clue.

"Dammit, what does that make me, and all the other females in a wheelchair? Less than a women?"

I now knew Patty was angry. No, Patty was pissed. Words like dammit did not come easily to her. This was something she really felt very strongly about.

"That is really bullshit!" Wow, big time pissed.

And here she was years later, a professional person as a dietitian, a homemaker, and a wife with two beautiful children.

And in a wheelchair.

A whole person.

"I've often wondered how that girl is doing," she said.

I shook my head in acknowledgement. Then I asked her to please write, if she would, what her experience at Southwest had meant to her and to be somewhat specific in regards to basketball.

She spent the next hour or so writing. We would visit periodically until she looked at me and asked if she could finish it later on after thinking about it.

I wasn't about to turn her down.

Sure enough, later that evening she pushed up to me handed me an envelope and muttered something about hoping it was what I wanted. Silly lady, anything was going to be 'alright' from her.

She shared with me:

When I came to SSU I had been in a chair for only nine months. I was involved in a car accident in December of my senior year resulting in a spinal cord injury. Prior to my accident, I had been involved in high school sports. I had height and could jump well and enjoyed a successful and enjoyable involvement. But I was green when I came to SSU. I met another girl who encouraged me to join the team. So I got in touch with you. You became, as I like to put it, like a second dad to me. You encouraged me to 'Go for it,' not to give up, to take what I had and make the very most of it. I still remember you telling me that at some time I would fall out of my chair and that I needed to learn how to get back in it. God, that scared me, because being a paraplegic, I couldn't even get up and down a curb by myself. The other players helped me learn. I remember once when I was trying to learn to 'pop' a wheelie and get up and down a curb, I fell out of my chair, just as you said I would. No one seemed to know what I had done wrong, but someone remarked I sure fell gracefully. Today people marvel at me, being a mother and a dietitian, but I think, "Gosh, it's what any normal person would do."

The Best Team No One Knows.

SSU Broncos: The Best Team No One Knows About—Dana Yost, Sports Editor. This was the headline of the sports page of our local newspaper. Two players and myself had been interviewed. There was an accompanying picture of me standing between the two players, they being in chairs and me holding a basketball.

I was having a cup of coffee in my office reading the article. Over the years there had been many, many articles about our games and about the program in general. There had developed a certain amount of skepticism on my part. For one thing more than a few of the articles were not found on the sports page, but on the personal feature or family page. The sports story would get lost in the sideshow of courage and obstacle hurtling of the individual players. The athleticism seemed to get lost. As more than one player shared with me, "Until the public realizes the chair is the vehicle, not THE story, disabled sports will be relegated to the feature page, and not the sports page."

As I read, this particular one seemed well balanced, about some of the team's frustrations but also about the positive aspects, the real joys. It was also on the sports page.

After some opening remarks attributed to me about playing to empty stands and how people were missing an outstanding basketball team, there was a direct quote from me, "Sometimes I think that maybe this is what college athletics should be, for the people involved, and if other people want to take advantage, so much the better."

I know that given today's' emphasis on big time sports, this is wishful thinking. Not very realistic. I would love to fill the stands with other than family, friends and a few curious individuals, some just waiting for the game to be over so they can have the time for open gym.

The two players in the picture were the team captains. They pointed out early in the article that we were lucky to have a hundred fans attend our games. I might add that this estimate may be too high; maybe fifty would be more accurate.

One captain was quoted, "You know its kinda funny, we are 18–3 and we've got the most realistic chance of winning a national title of any team on campus, but other teams get more attention. Maybe that's the way it should be. We can keep our focus more than the other teams. That's not a slam—but maybe it's motivating us a little bit more."

He then cautioned the readers not to confuse this with pity or sour grapes. Both players had pointed out that historically the Broncos had won eight consecutive conference championships and three national intercollegiate wheelchair basketball titles. The kids were proud of these accomplishments.

They also discussed that we practiced hard for two hours a day and worked to get better. This was athletics.

The article then shifted gears. In addition, the articles pointed out that not only were the players dealing with their own personal set of circumstances, but their coaches. This was alluding to yours truly. A year earlier I had gone through alcohol treatment after a divorce of some twenty-five years of marriage. To say I did not handle the situation well would indeed be a gross understatement. Anyone who has experienced one or both or similar situations can speak volumes as to the pain and loss of self.

The article alluded to, "Some off season turbulence over the past year or so," in reference to me. This was being humane and kind. Turbulence hell.

The captains spoke of their support and that in general they were some of my most ardent supporters. My feeling is that I believe their own individual trial and tribulations seemed to give them the sensitivity to feel my agony and frustrations, my imperfections, my humanness.

Without this support I often wonder what today might be, if at all. As one of my alumni told me when he visited me at the treatment center, "Hell Lew, you have helped many people in the past, it is time you allowed someone to help you." I think I had a glimmer into their world and they seemed to sense this. We struggle together. There is real strength in this. It just takes some of us longer to learn. What goes around comes around.

No fans, no recognition.

But we are more than OK.

P.S.—We did not win the national title. Perhaps if this had been a movie, but it wasn't, it was real life.

And nobody guaranteed life was going to be easy or fair.

Before he graduated Scott VanDerMillen, one of the captains wrote:

As I thought about the question that you asked me Lew, about what I believe that intercollegiate athletics did for me, the opportunity it gave me. As I stop to think about it, I think about it in terms of three things. Number one, I think that it taught me self-discipline in my life on and off the playing floor. As a college student, you tend to sometimes get caught up in the freedom that college life offers you and that goes hand-in-hand with athletics and oftentimes, athletic becomes more important than going to college itself and the distinct purpose in going to college sometimes gets out of focus. I think intercollegiate athletics offered me the opportunity to find self-discipline, to understand what self-discipline was, to become a very good time management type person.

The second thing that I think it did for me was to offer me a chance to grow as an individual in terms of relating with and to people because obviously, you have to be able to communicate with teammates, coaches and it really gives you an identity. I think athletics offers that to everyone. It did that for me as well. Growing as an individual, especially at the age of 18 to 20, I think is very important in getting involved in something on campus. It's very important, especially when you come from so far from home as I did myself and with there not being very many opportunities out there to be involved in intercollegiate athletics as Southwest State offers you. I think that that was a real golden opportunity for myself to take advantage of.

The third thing that I think about that it did for me was, it offered me an opportunity to challenge myself daily, not only athletically, but also academically, spiritually. It really made me step back and take a look at how different instances, different situations really relate to one another; how athletics goes hand-in-hand with how you conduct yourself in the 'real world.'

Those three things, self-discipline, being able to grow as an individual and then challenge myself daily, were very important to me and very vital to me as I wanted to become an educator, a teacher-coach person and my ability to be involve in and to learn from the opportunity that was granted me of the intercollegiate athletics at Southwest State, It was very a good foundation for my success. It laid some very important groundwork and obviously, you take advantage of an opportunity. Once the foundation is set, then you, as an individual, can build on that. I think I utilized that opportunity to build on that foundation that South-west State offered me

Ever Think About Killing Yourself?

"Ever think about killing yourself?"

A young high school student asked this question to one of the players. Period-ically, the team and I would visit a local high school for an awareness day. This usually involved visiting several classes, introducing the players who would 'tell their stories.' These sessions would be followed by a question and answer period.

Myself and six players had just completed the 'show and tell' part of the pro-gram and the questions had been rather normal and of a superficial variety about the problems of being disabled, about dating or having a boyfriend or girlfriend, career goals, and so forth. One student did ask about getting hurt and wondering if drinking had been involved. This question or discussion arose every so often and it was interesting over the years how many people had to answer in the affir-mative...lots of drinking and tough consequences.

The death question caught us by surprise and for the moment there was silence. I think I saw some embarrassment from the young lady who asked the question. I saw her motion with a shrug of her shoulders to a friend as if to say she was sorry she asked. She then blurted out, "Well it just popped into my head," by way of an apology." She was squirming and fidgeting in her chair.

She started to say something else when one of the players spoke, "I'll answer that."

I looked down the line. It seems we always lined up in front of the class, seemed to be the way to do this, I guess. The answer had come from Troy down at the opposite end from me.

Troy was a slightly built young man. He had been hurt in a motorcycle acci-dent around age sixteen. As I remember the story, he was not expected to live and was in a coma for several weeks. He did recover, but a neck injury had left him a quadriplegic.

My impression of him during his first couple of years at Southwest was one of struggle. He seemed bitter and distant, staying pretty much to himself. I didn't get to know him until early in his junior year when he expressed an interest in wheelchair basketball.

He became a real asset. His personality and outlook on life was very positive with a great sense of humor. It was a real pleasure to be around him. I had really misjudged him. He let me know very quickly that he was independent and would not tolerate being treated different. He knew that his functional level precluded him from being as he put it, "a stud," but he wanted to contribute what he could, on his terms. All this came out during one of our early meetings in my office. He was not shy. I grew to appreciate his honesty and candor.

I think this was one of his first experiences as an athlete. Some of his comments lead me to believe that he was not enamored with 'jocks' and 'jock society' as he would put it. No matter, he was a neat addition to our team.

After he responded to the young ladies question, there was another pause. I can remember thinking this question raised some awareness in me and I found myself thinking, "Could I personally deal with such a devastating or catastrophic accident?" This was not the first time this thought had crossed my mind. I had often told others and myself that I thought I could deal with being a paraplegic, with the use of both arms and hands. But to be a high level quad, or with a multiple disability is something else and, to me, an interesting question. I guess I thought that having worked with individuals with so many different disabilities would have given me, lets see, what? Maybe I had some insight or skill to cope where others would not and maybe I don't. Obviously, I have never nor hope to have the occasion to find out.

"To answer your question in a hurry, hell yes I thought about it, but I couldn't," he offered with a good deal of emotion. "Most people could not or would not ask such a question," he continued, "they are embarrassed or do not want to offend me with such matters. They seem to want to protect me. As though I cannot deal with such an issue. You or no one can protect me; I'm not a little child. As a matter of fact, I'm pretty damn tough," he concluded.

A hush would not accurately describe the room. There was silence.

He paused, leaned forward in his chair a bit and for a moment seemed to be thinking where he wanted to go next. He suddenly sat back up. He knew. "Trying to protect me robs me of my dignity. I have the right to solve and deal with my problems. So it's OK to ask me what you are really thinking. I'll tell you and let you know if I don't care to answer. You bet, I spent a lot of time feeling sorry for myself and crying, cursing God, or anything or anybody else I could blame. I went through all the stages of denying, anger, finally reaching the lowest point in my life after about six or seven months where I was so depressed I would have done anything to die. But as I said, I couldn't and in time I realized I wanted to live. Don't totally know when or how it happened. I'm not sure, but at some point I did make that decision. There have been times since then that thought has crept back, but Thank God, I did no act."

I noticed some of the other team members shaking their heads in agreement and could almost read their minds. It was as though they were saying, "Go Troy, go baby go."

Troy seemed to almost by instinct pick up on this and once again, without too much hesitation said, "Probably, many of us wanted to die, so sure, I wanted to die."

"Why didn't you?" the young lady asked.

I thought this was one great young lady; she is going to do all right in the world.

And Troys' answer came swiftly, "Because I couldn't. I was sandwiched between two mattresses in a frame that turned me over and over. I never fully understood all about why, but I was pinned in between them and couldn't move. Being a quad didn't help much either. I really, really wanted to die for a long time, but I just physically could not do it."

The session really opened up.

Towards the end, Troy once again spoke, "To finish my answer concerning suicide, believe me when I tell you that you can not imagine the depth of my depression. My life was over. What good was I in this condition? It took me a long time, a very long time to begin to really want to live and not just survive. Again, Thank God I could not or did not act on my thoughts."

I thought we were done and started to say something when another question was asked, by whom I wasn't sure, but it was very direct, "How about dating, you-know, and, uh, sex and how long does it take you to get dressed, do you have help?"

I looked at Troy and said, "Be my guest."

"Wow, let's see, and let me answer the last part first. No I don't need help but it takes me an hour or so to shit, shower and shave in the morning. And thank God for Velcro, it's the greatest thing since sliced bread. My bowel and bladder program would take too long to explain, but again, I'm independent."

He seemed to take a deep breath, paused for a moment looking as if he were trying to think about what to say next and he finally just seemed to blurt out, Sex, great subject," and then after another pause, "Can I get it up? Yeh. With some help, which I won't go into but if you're really curious, see me after we finish." The last was said with an impish grin, or maybe it was some other kind.

That did end the session.

6

Impact

John shares.

I finally cornered John Schatzlein at his home several years after he had graduated, after he was married, with two lovely girls. I stuck a small recorder in his
hand and just, in essence said, go, tell me in your own words what it meant to be
a Bronco or what you are feeling about the experience after these many years."
These then, are his words as best as I transcribed:

First of all, competition was very much a pert of my life, prior to my injury. It
was a positive sense of competition. I felt fairly comfortable. I was considered to
be a fairly competent athlete.

When I was fourteen years old, and just beginning to compete at a higher level
I was pretty well established. When I acquired my spinal cord injury, which was
caused by falling out of a tree—somewhere between fifty and sixty feet high. I
think there was a sense of competition going on at that time. The tree was tall. It
was high, and I knew that I could climb it. Height wasn't an issue. Competition
was something that I did every day, whether it was with the neighborhood kids or
whether it was in the team way. For me it was just a matter of seeing the challenge of that big tree and deciding to climb it.

When I first acquired the injury, I didn't want to hear that I was going to be
paralyzed. I didn't want to know that all of the other part of my life—to that
extent—would be over, especially as it relates to athletics and things like that.
Needless to say, we know that is not accurate, But I wasn't able to hear anybody
at that time. There were several months where I really didn't want to work out. I
really didn't want to work hard. I didn't really care whether I lived or died
because I didn't think that I could grow up to be what I had thought I might
have to be. I had no real sense of what I thought I had to be, but I knew that it
had to do with not being paralyzed from the 'waist down.'

119

Once I did get through that and they started to challenge me in the hospital...After I got out of the hospital, which ended up being like about eight months in 1963, I immediately continued in the competition element in that I had to go back into the community and prove that I was still okay.

However, I felt much better in appearance on the outside than I really felt on the inside. While I looked like I was coping with the disability and dealing with it well, inside I was struggling to feel okay about whether I could fit into an able-bodied world, that really very obviously said it wasn't okay to have some form of disability or functional limitation.

In trying to close the concept of competition and athletics in my college experiences, it was a combination of benefits. One benefit was that I could feel good about being involved in the development of something that was never there. So, in helping develop programs that provided greater opportunities for the students that followed behind me. In one sense it was the greatest part of the competition because you were trying to instill a philosophy and a concept in an academic institutional environment that heretofore had never thought about the inclusion of persons with mobility impairments or disabilities in as a significant way as has been accomplished. The sense of being able to know that I did contribute to any of the athletic teams that I participated in—be it basketball or track and field, or whichever event I participated in was really secondary to me.

Although I think that we spend too much time in providing alkaloids to the athletes that have super talent and super skills, and don't spend enough time providing positive feedback and rewards to the persons who are middle-class and middle road skill people...Competition is kind of an anomaly in terms—in that we think of it in negative terms. But more often than not, it is very a positive kind of thing...Positive competition is essential to skill development and negative competition can destroy one's self-esteem and personal sense of value at the expense of somebody else.

The Kid.

The season was over. Marks' wheelchair basketball career was over at Southwest. I had been a very good four years, for the team and for him individually. He had 1,566 career points with participation on a national intercollegiate championship or two and some most valuable player awards from our team as well as national recognition.

Mark and I were in the therapy room. He was rocked back in his chair against a wall watching me work out with a pair of dumbbells—very light dumbbells. I had been 'working out', 'pumping iron' when he rolled in.

"Remember my freshman year?" he asked.

"Mark, I remember the first day you pushed into the therapy area," I responded.

"You know," he replied, "I remember that very well."

We both sort chuckled.

He continued, "I still hear that first word from you—Mortenson."

I nodded in agreement.

"Mortenson," you barked as I pushed by you. "God, I stopped dead in my tracks. Even then your voice scared hell out of me and was my command," Mark shared with me, with a smile on his face. Then you said, "Get that name off the back of your chair, you're not the KID any more, you're Mark Mortenson."

I again nodded as I recalled the leather strap, about six inches in width across the upper back of his chair with THE KID burnt in big letters across it.

"I remember," he continues after a brief pause, "you didn't suggest, you didn't hint, you demanded and it scared hell out of me."

"Sorry'bout that," I said. We both knew I was kidding.

"No, it was OK. Before coming to Southwest I attended high school, but there were no programs for little spina bifs like me. I just went to study hall for PE. Anyway, I started playing ball for the local, community team. As you know, even this was more recreational, but I met you and you got me interested in coming to Southwest—I mean, here was a wheelchair sports program and I know that kept me in college for the first year or so. Basically, I had never thought of myself as a college graduate or even a college student."

Once again I nodded, in agreement and countered, "I recall watching you play on that team. I knew you had potential when I saw how quick you were, even back in high school."

Our conversation trailed off for a few moments. Mark watched as I finished a set of curls with the dumbbells. One thing at a time you know. I caught my breath and looked at him. I think he thought I was going to have a heart attack.

"I still remember that dumb name, THE KID," I finally said after regaining enough oxygen, "burnt into that piece of leather attached to the back of your chair. I also noticed that this was the way you were treated. On that team, your role was to pass the ball as soon as you got it and then go pick for the others so they could shoot."

"Hey," he said, "what did I know?"

"Yeh, I understand," I agreed, "your first year here was really a wake up call for you. I won't forget you spent almost two years of, who me shoot?"

"Hell, no one had ever told me to shoot for Gods' sake. I was confused. I had never been allowed to shoot before."

I grinned at him and said, "Yep, I know. Remember the time in one of your early games here when I called time out and chewed you up one side and down the other for passing up a little six footer?"

"Damn, remember," he said, "I was petrified, no one had ever chewed me out like that."

"Yeh, you did have a stunned, dumb look on your face. Actually, to be real honest now, I can tell you I actually felt sorry for you, but had decided I need to get up in your face."

"God, Lew, I really didn't know what to do. I wanted to find a hole and crawl in it and cry, quit, anything. And my mom and dad were behind you cheering you on, not that you needed any encouragement. I mean, my own flesh and blood. That is something I'll never forget."

"But bless your little pea-pickin' heart, you shot the ball the next time," I reminded him.

"Yep, and I went through my sophomore and junior year asking myself, when do I shoot and finally my senior year of, yeh, you bet, just let me have the ball to shoot.

It was interesting seeing you go from THE KID to an almost college graduate of today," I responded. "Just like a grown person."

He rocked forward settling his chair back on the floor and shook his head, and no words were necessary, I understood what he meant.

As he began to leave, I said, "You were one of the first basketball players I had ever had to beg to shoot. Hell, most of the rest always thought they were some manifestation of an NBA star."

A few years later in reply to my request, the KID wrote the following:

Before coming to Southwest, I was attending high school in Sioux Falls and I started playing basketball with the Sioux Wheelers. It was in a way more of a rec-reational activity. Looking back at it, I thought I was going to learn something about the game, but it did get me interested in going to Southwest for the basic reason that there was a wheelchair sports program there, and I think that is what kept me in college, basically.

I came to Southwest as an accounting major and found out my first year into the quarter that I wasn't really prepared for accounting. I had little math back-ground and I was trying to take all these algebra and trig courses that I had no idea about. I was beginning to get where I wanted to leave school—then I heard this voice say, "No, change your major." So I did and became a history major and my academics improved greatly, I'd say and I think my being involved with the Bronco's was a major part because if that hadn't have been there I probably would have dropped out of school and gone onto something else.

It made me grow up, it made me become more independent, more responsible for my actions. There was no Mother, no Father around to tell you what to do. You could go to class, not go to class, that was an option. If you did not go to class, you paid the consequences. You could go to practice. If you didn't do that you would pay consequences. Being involved was really a motivational factor, it gave you something to feel good about and in order to do that, you had to maintain your eligibility, you had to keep your grades, you had to take certain classes and you had to get your degree basically.

250 lb. Teddy Bear.

(Ten, nine, eight...)

Shit, we're not going to get a shot.

I had called a time out with fifteen seconds to go in the first half. I had outlined a play on my coach's handy-dandy magnetic board with its red and blue little magnetic buttons. I went over the play at least twice. All the players in the huddle shook their heads in acknowledgement.

It is at time like this I always felt like I was a coach, a coach who really understood the game and how to depart this vast knowledge to the players.

At the end of the timeout, the team formed a circle, pushing their chairs in towards me with each player holding hands with those on either side of them. We counted to three and all yelled, 'Southwest'. The players then broke the huddle and returned to the floor for action.

I was proud, just another indication of my coaching discipline and organizational prowess. I somewhat jest, but these things do add an air to my own perceived importance of coaching.

I was about, once again, to be reminded just how wrong or what an illusion this is.

As soon as my team took the floor for the throw in, one of the players was completely out of position. I thought, "God, he is not only physically disabled, but also brain dead." No amount of yelling of screaming made any difference. Even when I called upon the Almighty for guidance was there any response. He was petrified and frozen in time and space.

In came the ball. Utter confusion. The clock started its countdown.

(seven, six, five)

The ball was now in the hands of my little darling who had screwed up my magnificent play. I was screaming, "Shoot, shoot."

He was at least twenty-five feet, with his back to the basket and with no clue as to what to do. This was before the three-point line, so it did not matter where a player shot the ball. It was worth only two points.

(four, three, two)

In what I'm sure was in absolute terror and sheer desperation he launched a hook shot where he imagined the basket to be. He absolutely couldn't see it sitting where and how he was sitting on the floor.

(one, and the horn. Half over)

The ball was still in the air. It never hit anything but the backboard and down through the net. A bank shot from twenty-five feet and it was good.

Unbelievable. There is a God!

My players were all celebrating, pushing around and 'high fiving'. I told my manager to get the team into the locker room and at the same time motioned to my little hero to come over to me.

His head and eyes dropped down to the floor as he slowly, very slowly pushed his way over to me. He reminded me of myself as a small boy, having to face my mother when I had done something wrong.

When he reached me I said rather casually, "Nice shot." "What?" He asked in a startled voice. "Nice shot," I repeated.

His eyes were wide, in a fear like look and in rapid fire he blurted, "I was feeling your hot breath on my neck. I just knew I had screwed up and was scared not to score. You can't believe how scared I was." "Sure I can," I replied.

Big Ross Martin had come into wheelchair basketball with very little experience in any sport. He had a condition that was so rare as to be found in only a few families. I was never sure of what it was, but it left Ross lacking in stamina plus uncoordinated with some visual problems.

When he first became aware he was eligible for wheelchair basketball, due the neurological impairment, he was unsure about, "This wheelchair stuff." One particular feeling he shared with me that I've always remembered was that he lacked self-confidence and had no sense of self-respect. He always considered himself to be an observer, not a participant of life.

In high school he was, in his words, "Allowed to be the manager in basketball." He noticed so-called handicapped individuals were repeatedly the managers because of the disability. He grew up believing he could not be an athlete. "After all," he said, "if you're told something often enough and long enough, you begin to believe it. It becomes reality." He saw this as an issue of pity and there was some bitterness in his words.

This changed when he entered the world of wheelchair basketball. His world was turned upside down. At first, in practice, people would dominate him, intimidate him and physically push him around.

I watched all this as it unfolded. At least I watched for a few practices. Finally, with no change, I had watched all I could. I stopped practice one day during a scrimmage and in my very best gym voice and own inimitable coaching technique, I yelled, "Dammit Ross, you're 250 pounds and you just let a little smurf take the ball away from you."

I could tell, no one had ever yelled at him like this. His look and body language was like a small puppy with its tail between its legs. "Ross," I continued, "you are a 250 pound teddy bear. You're the biggest bear in the woods, for Gods' sake, get tough. Hell, growl at somebody."

This was the beginning of two or three intense weeks for Ross. I made the decision to push him—hard. I was on his butt for every mistake. My dad always strongly suggested that if I was going to chew on people, I need to praise them when they deserve it. Don't be just negative. Sometimes this is not an easy task. Ross wasn't doing too many things well.

Sorta like good cop—bad cop.

I wasn't sure how Ross would respond but decided to continue.

There were times I wondered if such verbal abuse and toughness, which at time bordered on the cruel, was going to work or even if it was appropriate. I realize some players are not only turned off by this treatment, but they will rebel. They may give up and quit. Ross and I were working hard.

Yes, the teddy bear began to respond. He was becoming an athlete. The pride and joy that comes with this development is absolutely amazing.

So, here we were, still sitting out in the bench area after the 'miracle' shot. We seemed to be suspended in our own little time warp, each, I'm sure with many memories.

I finally said, "Let's go to the locker room."

He looked up at me and said in a rather light manner, "Notice, I used the backboard. You always told me the backboard cost lots of money and we should use them. See, I did listen to you."

I shook my head and smiled.

He reached out and laid his hand on my forearm and said, "I want to thank you for believing in me. I'm actually a force to be reckoned with."

Gotta tell you, I chocked up a bit. My eyes were a wee bit teary as we exchanged acknowledging nods.

No words were necessary.

I often wondered what Ross would relate when I asked him to write about the Broncos and his experience. He seemed to have a tough time. When I would see him over the years he would always tell me he, "Wanted to get it right." It took him several years, so I was anxious to read his words:

It has been several years since I played in my last organized wheelchair basketball game. Since then I have spent many hours thinking about what I actually learned from my time with the Southwest State Broncos. I have many wonderful memories, a couple of thrilling stories, and several thousand humorous anecdotes. It has taken a long time for me to get to a point in life where I could put my thoughts down on paper; so here I go.

I first became involved with wheelchair athletics during my freshman year in college. That is when I started playing wheelchair basketball for the Broncos. I was out of shape, overweight. I lacked self-confidence, but most of all I had no sense of self-respect. I had always considered myself an observer of life, not a participant of life.

Now, some years later I find that to no longer be the case. I look back at that so called adult that I appeared to be and am amazed that I am where I am today. I have a wonderful wife, a remarkable little boy, and a job that I truly enjoy.

What I got out of playing wheelchair basketball is actually a life that is worth living. Wheelchair basketball taught me that I am actually a force to be reckoned with. Basketball taught me that I do have gifts that are a worthwhile contribution to the group. Playing ball has given me the tools to adapt to outside conditions as well as react to the actions of others. I learned to think about the future, and know I myself have to help determine its outcome. Of all the things that I learned the one that I cherish the most is the self-determination that is achieved in 'normal' competition. Through basketball, I achieved control of one aspect of my life, and because of this I was able to use this control to change the rest of my life.

I have memories of exhilarating wins, as well as heartbreaking losses. I have set goals for myself; attained these goals, and in some cases gone far beyond the goals I set. Through competition with others I became an adult. I learned about myself as well as others. I developed pride, self-worth and self-confidence. It really amazes me how much a single person can learn within a team sport.

To this day, whenever I am in a gymnasium, or when I pick up a basketball, I remember all the work, joy and even the love that wheelchair basketball brought me. Those things are the intangible aspects that everyone seeks in normal competition. I received those things from playing with the Broncos. After all, the real important things are not what you achieve while you are competing. The important things are what you bring away from the contest and carry with you the rest of your life.

And then there was Peggy.

"Hi coach, got a minute?"

"For you, always."

Peggy had stepped into my office after tapping on the open door jam. "You know I'm transferring after this year. Southwest doesn't have a therapeutic major."

"I'm going to miss you, but I heard and I wish you well. I'm excited for you."

"I just wanted to say goodbye and share a few thoughts."

I stopped doing whatever it was I was doing and said, "Let's go down to the student union for a cup of coffee or whatever. I'm buying."

"You're buying? I like that. Make mine a coke. I'll meet you down there."

I got my cup of coffee and her coke, paid the cashier and found us a table. Peggy dallied for a few minutes greeting a friend with some small talk.

I was turning my coffee cup in my hand as she joined me at the table. She had a slight limp from a cerebral palsy condition. Otherwise, except for a very slight slurring of her speech, one would not realize she had a disability. She had been involved in high school track, as she would say, "able-body style." I first saw her playing wheelchair basketball on a women's team from the Minneapolis—St Paul area. I recruited her during her junior and senior year in high school.

She separated from her friend, came over and sat down saying; "I want to thank you for the opportunity. It has been a really good feeling to be treated like a student-athlete."

"The pleasure was all mine," I replied, with a big, dumb grin on my face.

"Ya, right. You're full of it. But anyway, the fact that I limped uh made it tough for some people like teachers and coaches to come down hard on me. They were afraid to correct me."

"Like me, huh."

"You are full of it, but we both know that. Hey, a lot of people are pretty alarmed that a person could yell at a poor person with a limp or in a chair."

"Are you suggesting I yelled at you?" I feigned being hurt.

"Ha," she grunted.

We both grinned!!!

"I had heard about you, but I don't know I was ready for your practices. That was a real shocker for me. I learned two rules from you. Remember what they were?" she asked.

"Wow, I give, what words of wisdom did I impart?"

"I didn't say words of wisdom. I said rules," she said emphatically. "Still don't remember?"

"Nope."

"There were two rules you wanted me to know. I think it was because I was a girl, which pissed me off in the beginning. I thought you were a sexist pig. I learned later I was right."

I looked at her over my spectacles and cut in at this point, "Are you going to tell me or are you going to continue with this sexist thing? I'll admit to being a sexist pig if it helps you get to the point."

"OK, OK," she said, "You told me that rule number one was that basketball players don't cry and that rule number two was always to remember rule number one."

"Yeh, what a beast."

"I gotta tell you that there were times when you really were a jerk," she said as she looked me in the eye, "you were demanding and your language—wow. It was sure different. I was in a cultural shock. No one really prepares you for any of this, especially when you have been sheltered much of your life."

"Well kiddo," I said, "just between you and I, I sometimes do wonder. I know my language is tough for some people to take, not to mention how demanding I am for some people. OK, I can read your mind," I quickly added, seeing she was about to react, "a lot of people! Maybe I need to soften. I don't know, maybe I feel others pain and relate to each person."

Wow, what BS," she interjected.

"Hey, let me finish." I was just pausing to see if you were paying attention. "But, naw, you wouldn't know me and love me the way you do if I change, right?"

Peggy slid back in her chair, laughing and answered, "Maybe sometimes. I think you are rather hard on yourself, harder than anyone else. And who are you kidding, you change? But I want to thank you for treating me like an athlete, one of the guys so to speak. It's been a blast."

"You've been great. Wow, we sound like a mutual admiration society," I said.

"That's OK, I'll always be a Bronco at heart." Before you leave would you do me a favor?" I asked. "Write me a page or two about your feelings and what you experienced. I would really appreciate it."

"I'll try to remember, just like your two rules," she said. And with that she got up, blew me a kiss and waved goodbye.

A week later she stopped by my office and handed me an envelope. "Here's your request for my feelings."

I took the envelope and thanked her. And with my thanks she was gone. I waited, turned the envelope over several times, but curiosity got she best of me. There was some trepidation, what with Peggy' honest nature, but what the hell. I took the material and read:

I was involved in my junior high seventh and eighth grade softball team and played wheelchair basketball in 1984. I started and I played wheelchair basketball with the Rolling Gophers, and then I was involved in my high school track team for able-bodied. I threw shot put and discus.

The first thing I noticed when I went to Southwest was that I felt very comfortable with the fact that I could use my chair. The campus was accessible. Growing up it had always been no, don't use your chair, you should walk. I really felt more comfortable using my chair, and just being able to express who I was. Sometimes I needed to use it. Sometimes I wanted to use it. I wasn't allowed to at home. Where I grew up wasn't accessible. The attitudes that people had—you know—there are not that many people in wheelchairs. I think they thought that I was making fun of people that really needed or were in chairs all the time, because I could walk.

I think it was a really good feeling to be a student-athlete, because I had seen other people who went off to college that were student-athletes and really admired how they were able to adjust their time schedules and their study habits to maintain the GPA's that were required and practice and put in as much practice time they needed to. I thought it would be a real challenge to do that—to get my study skills down—so I could attend classes and go to play basketball and go to basketball tournaments and still have time to do things with friends, and just all the things that you do in college including getting a job or whatever.

I found it real useful because I was able to do that. I kept a pretty good grade average. I think that being involved in so many things helped me to use my time more wisely and it just made me more aware of things that I could do.

I really enjoyed playing on the male basketball team being one of only two females. I had always been a tomboy and to me it didn't matter. I thought it was really funny, and you could just see—they would forget that there were two females on the bus. They would start whistling at the girls out the window and talk about girls. I would just blush. I thought it was the funniest thing in the world. They never treated me any different than one of the guys, so for that it was really good.

As far as competition, I was in my own way. I wasn't physically strong as some of the players, but as far as knowledge of the game and a kind of sense of the floor and rules—where to be and what kinds of things that need to be done, a court sense, I think I had that down. It didn't really bother me that I didn't play as much as some of the guys on the team because we were playing other teams that were male teams. I would get put in and they would say, "Hey, there is a girl." The other teams were always bigger, stronger, and taller. It was real interesting to see. I enjoyed watching and cheering, as well as playing. I think that I had enough to contribute to the team. They asked me, "What should I do here, where should I be?" I think that was good.

The fact that I limped a lot of coaches were afraid to come down on me and afraid to yell at me, or tell me that I was doing something incorrectly because they didn't know if it was because I physically couldn't do it or that I didn't know how. Some of the time was that I just didn't know. I was doing what I knew and they weren't talking the time to say—your form is incorrect or whatever.

I think, as a wheelchair athlete, more and more people are beginning to see that people in wheelchair athletics are no different than any other athlete. They train just as hard as any other athlete, they train so many hours per day, or whatever. Their diet is usually similar to that of any other—say, an able-bodied basketball team is training. They need to keep the same academic requirements.

Therefore, there is not a real difference in the way you coach, other than a technique or form or the fact that you have to coach a wheelchair basketball team. You talk about the rules in wheelchair basketball, rather than rules of something else.

I think that in general, they should be treated and seen as 'normal athletes.' A lot of people are pretty alarmed that a person could yell at a poor person in a wheelchair, and I don't know how to tell them that they should be yelled at or talked to or something—if they are not doing something correctly. It is the only way that they are going to get better. That is their goal. They want to be the best wheelchair basketball player they could be or whatever. The only way they can do this is by practice and by making mistakes and getting corrected.

That Jerk.

Mark came into the student union, spotted me and with a big grin on his face and pushed over to my table. I was having a cup of coffee between classes. I could tell he was excited about something.

"Got a moment?" he asked as he neared me. "Sure," I replied. "What can I do for you?"

He was a pretty good-sized young man with reddish hair and a young looking face. He was a para, another motorcycle accident. It seemed we had our share and then some when it came to motorcycles. Mark was a real disaster, waiting to happen, as he was very accident-prone. At an earlier age he had cut off one of his thumbs, poked him self in the eye with a stick, impairing his vision and a few other mishaps that I learned about over his time at Southwest. Evidently he was a risk taker, and seemed to identify himself as somewhat of a rebel, and as I was to experience, not too fond of authority. He and I clashed his first few months. Actually it was more like war and some hardheadedness on both our parts.

He did not play any sports in high school. In addition to being a para, he was a farm boy and that took up most of his free time. One of the first recollections I have of him was watching him shoot for the first time. I've seen blacksmiths with better touches, good thing our backboards were well made.

Our relationship had grown over time and he was becoming a friend in addition to the basketball floor. He was a bright young man; a business Administration Major, quick with his wit and all in all had a pleasant personality, when he wasn't fighting the world.

"Lew," he said, still with the big grin on his face, "I gotta tell you something. Remember how you and I fought each other for a while. I thought you were the biggest dip-shit, and told you so, and you called me a'yo-yo'?"

"What do you mean used to?" I cut in, but with a grin of my own.

"Ya, ya," he continued, "I just had a great conversation with one of my instructors. I told him we were leaving next Thursday for a road trip and needed to know if it would be OK to miss Friday and if so what did I have to do? At first he was pissed, accusing wheelchair basketball of interfering with our academic pursuits and how that it was a bunch of bull. I assured him this was not going to happen often and that is why I was seeing him early, that this was a request and not an ultimatum. He liked that. We talked a bit about my assignment."

"God, this is getting long," I once again interjected.

"I'm getting there, hold your horses, and don't be in such a hurry."

"I've got class in thirty minutes," I said facetiously.

"Hell, your students won't care if you don't show up," he countered. He was quick. So I shut up to let him continue.

"Anyway, as I started to leave his office and I won't mention his name, he asked me how I got along with you. He said he had seen one of our practices and heard you yelling and screaming at the players. He thought that in his opinion it was very demeaning and not the least bit cruel. I kinda shrugged it off and told him that even though you yelled, most of it was positive, but when we did something wrong, you let us know—as in right now."

"I'll bet you were snickering,"

"No, actually I found myself defending you," he continued. "That even surprised me. I just told him you were trying to make us better and whether I or anyone else agreed with your style, well that you were the coach. I did tell him that sometimes you have to tear down a lot of walls and attitudes before you can build up a lot of them."

He paused.

Before I could add something he continued, "I would be lying to you if I said that here were no times I thought, God what a jerk Lew is. But after awhile I began to even appreciate that you were treating me no different. To be really truthful I was kinda proud."

"And what did your instructor think or say to all this gibberish?" I asked.

Mark just smiled and added, "He just shook his head and grunted something about he still thought you were an SOB. He didn't buy into it."

When I asked Mark to write his thoughts about the program a couple of years later he seemed almost eager. The thought crossed my mind that maybe he was going to take this opportunity for a 'payback'. After all by this time he was graduating and 'out of my clutches.' I would like to share a quick story about Mark and I. Mark was still round when my divorce occurred. I was devastated, drinking heavily, desperate—use any descriptor and I probable fit it. Mark insisted that I attend the National Wheelchair Basketball Tournament with him that spring down in Kansas City. I fought him, told him to leave me alone. All those things that tend to drive the people who you love and who love you away. He would not take no for an answer. We went. What this meant I don't know I'll ever totally understand. What I do know is Thank God he and others were there. We had come a long way.

His feelings were important to me and I read his writing with my heart up in my throat as I read:

One of the things that Bronco basketball has really bought to my life is the fact that teamwork actually works. I use it pretty much in every part of my life now, especially with playing other sports, but also in business. I have come to realize that teamwork is really worthwhile as far as getting things done. When I first started on the Broncos, it was actually kind of tough. I was pretty much of an individual person. I t was tough working with other people and learning how to play as a unit in defense and offense and it's really made a big difference. I took a lot of the teamwork outside of the Bronco Basketball program and used it in business. In business, we are constantly looking as far as defense on what the competitor is doing and also in offense, what the competitor is doing. I think it made a big difference knowing that if you work together with your salespeople and with other parts of business, you can get a lot done.

One of the other things that really made a difference is the many friendships that I have acquired over the years. I played with a lot of people in my four years, but I think the biggest thing is that most of the people that I've played with have been really good friends and we have kept together over the years, some more than others, but every time you see the ones that you played with, there's a history there. And the history is what everybody is all about. You look more towards the history than into the future and I think one of the things that I look at is that probably the strongest friendship I'll ever have were established in college on that basketball team, and you can almost ask any of them to do something for you and they will do it. I think that's very important.

(The next paragraph retold the story of the instructor who questioned him about me. When I read this, it was almost word for word with the conversation Mark and I had in the student union. We both remembered the incident right down to the reference to me being an SOB. What a coincidence, or is it?)

In closing, it's hard to separate Bronco basketball and Lew Shaver. It really is. We take a look at it and we call it Bronco basketball, but it is a fraternity and we look at Lew Shaver as the leader of the fraternity, more or less the president. He's had a lot of people come through his doors. You know, a lot of good people that have been very successful in life, both in terms of business, money, and everything else, but also a lot of people socially. You take a look at some of the things that John Schatzlein is doing and David Van Buskirk who works on the Alumni Committee and you go down the roll and there are pretty decent citizens all around. I think a lot of it has to do with playing for the Broncos. I think a lot of people that went through the program still look back, you know, when they come back for alumni day or if they see the Broncos play, when they're playing on other teams, you know, they still feel that they're part of the team. You know they always will be. It's no surprise that there's a lot of basketball players in the state of Minnesota, South Dakota, Wisconsin, that have played with Southwest State and are a big part of the basketball elite of Minnesota.

Coach I Need You On My Team.

It had been a tough year and it continued. We were at a weekend tournament and had just finished our first game. I was devastated. The night before a couple of our players had reportedly cut curfew, not by minutes, but by an hour or so. My curfew rule was rather simple. I would set a time, dependent on the situation with some input from the players, and in essence trust the players. I would give some responsibility to the team captains to coordinate, enforce, or whatever they thought was right to enforce the time.

To make matters worse, I only had five players for the weekend, so any disciplinary action would have been difficult without destroying the entire weekend.

At least that is what I rationalized. As a coach I hated these times. The old how could people do this to me bit? I know, I know, its what they are doing to themselves, but that is tough to swallow from time to time. I was angry and obviously feeling some self-pity.

The game we lost was in the morning. We were done by noon. So we had the rest of the afternoon and evening off. I probably should have scheduled something for the team. Ain't hindsight wonderful.

The game was absolutely terrible. No teamwork and halfhearted efforts and worse, to me, no desire.

One particular player was just going through the motions. He was a young freshman and as the kids labeled him, 'a lawsuit baby.' This was a nickname given to someone who had been in an accident as a baby or very young person. This young man had been about six when a drunk driver hit him while he was riding his bike on a bridge. This left him a paraplegic. He reportedly had gotten a huge settlement that guaranteed him around $4,000.00 a month for the rest of his life. He had all kinds of toys including a cabin on a local lake, a new truck almost every year, with a ten million dollar sound system that could be heard two area codes away, snowmobiles, and much, much more.

I'm not sure the price he paid was worth it. What I saw was a young man who really did not see the importance of a college education or needed wheelchair basketball for that matter. He was skilled with boundless potential. That bothered me as much as anything. It seemed a waste to me. Anyway, his effort, towards most things, was really laid back, a lack of any motivation or interest, including his classroom work and performance on the court.

Just all around lousy, a true 'bad hair' day in my humble opinion. The fun was gone. After thirty-plus years of coaching this group had done me in, maybe the old fire-in-the-belly was going out. Going out hell, I was drowning, gasping for a breath of air.

At half time, I gave no game strategy or adjustment talk. I simply told them that I had had it, that on Monday I would probably resign. Period.

About five minutes into the second half, I took the young player, who was still just going through the motions out of the game. Disabled or not, I was fed up with his attitude and chose to play with only four players while he cooled his butt on the bench. I really don't think he cared. I had never done anything like this before and had no idea how the others would respond.

To my surprise and delight, the team responded and actually played better without him. After a few minutes he pushed up to me and asked to go back in the game. I asked if he were really sure he wanted to play and he assured me he was. I looked at him and paused, sighed, and told him as honestly as I could that I didn't really give a shit if he ever played again, but to report back in.

Back in he went and we completed the game. Probably for the first time in my coaching career I just sat, said nothing and did nothing to help the kids in any way. Talk about catatonic.

Afterwards I walked out into a hallway, alone with my own thoughts, which were confused at best. I prided myself on having never quit. The old male macho, but I really felt whipped. I rationalized that if a group of disabled people could not care less and give up, why should I give a damn. To hell with it all.

I was staring out a window with no particular thought when Brenda pushed up to me. "Coach," she said, "I've been looking for you."

Brenda was a neat young lady. She was very bright, nice looking, and a most determined person. There had been several young ladies on our teams over the years. Most of the time they would not get to play much as their skill level and strength was not as good as many of the men. This is not any reflection on their desire, just an indication of the lack of opportunity to play anything when they were younger.

But Brenda had to play. We only had five or six players for the year. I kidded her all year about this saying, "You get to play whether you want to or not." She thrived on it, lived it.

I truly enjoyed her as a person and a player. She was a para due to spina bifida and seemed to have worked through many of the trials and tribulations of being disabled. Perhaps a teachers pet, or rather a coach's pet. I always told myself it was not because she was a girl, but because of her attitude.

She handed me a brown, paper sack and announced, "It's the only thing I could find to write on." Handing it to me, she pivoted her chair and pushed hurriedly away. I watch her go, then glanced down at the sack. She had written me a note. I thought that this was really different and it must be important. It read:

Dear Coach,

There are two things I would like to tell you about myself right now. The first is that I like to tell it how I see it, whether I'm right or wrong. I don't blow smoke up any ones' butt, so to speak. I'm very honest.

The second thing is that I don't like to listen sometimes. If I think I'm right, I tend to think it's the only way—you can ask my folks. I gave them a run for their money.

Someone, less than a week ago, said something to me. In these words, more or less they said, "Do the best you can, with what you have, wherever you are."

Our focus as a team many times is to 'keep our heads up in the game and not give up.

I came to Southwest for only ONE reason—to play wheelchair athletics. Maybe that was a bad choice. They didn't even have my major here. But I wanted to play. And I don't regret it in the least because I learned SO much from basketball about teamwork, cooperation, and TOLERATION.

This is not a letter to 'kiss up' or to 'beg and grovel.' This is SIMPLY to ask you to listen to your own words and to live by them as well as I have tried, though I throw the proverbial ball away time after time.

Coach, I admire you and I need you on my team. I just want you to know that.

As I finished reading, it occurred to me that sometimes we need to be reminded and it comes from the most unexpected and wonderful source.

Just a quick item. It was Brenda who really suggested the title of this book. So please blame her should you need to blame someone. I'm kidding. I think it was Mark Twain who said something to the effect that we should not take the blame for anything until we have exhausted all the other possibilities.

A few weeks later after the tough weekend, I gave an stack of stories to her to review as she was a English Major, a creative writer, plus she a member of the team. I wanted her opinion and input. After a couple of weeks she pushed into my office, plunked down the stories and informed me I had to finish this as she had never read anything like it about people with disabilities. She also informed me that I seemed to be trying to tell their story and not mine, and it was my story that was interesting. We discussed this for a bit and I agreed I needed to shift the emphasis basically to me. She suggested it was my feelings that were important.

She then asked about the title and I mumbled something about, *Opportunities*, to which she stuck her finger in her mouth and gagged. I called her a smart butt and asked what she had in mind. She began to relate the episode with Curt Kettner and his, "Yeh, Damn Bunch of Cripples," remark. I was taken aback a bit and inquired about the political correctness of such a title to which she responded, "Since when have you ever worried about political correctness?" A title was born!

The Best To Last.

Gotta' confess. This is one of the neatest episodes. I admit a definite partiality. Ever hear the phrase, "closet cripple?" This is a phrase to describe a person with a disability who, for whatever reason, does not or cannot accept the disability and literally closets themselves in their room, apartment, or home.

I'm not sure how wide spread the frequency is, or if it even exists, but if and when it does, it must be frightening and lonely as an existence.

One young man sure seemed to fit the description. Dick had been involved in a farm accident leaving him a high paraplegic. It is my impression he was in his late teens or so. When he came to Southwest a later he seemed to be any and very bitter although getting to know him initially was difficult. All this supposition may be totally erroneous, but it is my feeling.

I would only see him occasionally and then only fleetingly. He was a student in a wheelchair. This latter fact leads me to an effort to recruit him for the wheelchair basketball team.

No interest. At least that I could detect.

He was not disrespectful, said he just wasn't interested. He even thanked me for my interest. I continued to encourage him explaining that there were opportunities in addition to basketball in track and field, swimming, archery, weight lifting, and table tennis, all of which could lead to regional, national, and even international competition and travel.

He continued to show no interest, but also continued to be polite.

Some of the other players would ask if he talked or ever leave his room. Somebody remarked, "Hey, leave him alone, maybe he just wants it that way."

I never completely gave up on him, not that he needed me to play mother. I am persistent. I do try to be encouraging without being overbearing and excited without being silly. I am persistent. I seem to be repeating myself!

I think my persistence wore him down, but this may be an illusion or my ego speaking. Whatever the reason, he did, after a couple of months come to a few practices. He would sit and watch. But he was there. He would leave before we finished, but would resurface a practice or two later.

In the spring we were into our track and field practices. Dick had shown up during an earlier practice, but registered no interest in continuing.

One afternoon, a concerned professor in our science department stopped by my office, asking if I knew this particular student. I said I sure did.

My colleague proceeded to tell me of his concern. This kid was very bright and had a great deal of potential, but no one could get close to him. So, I should do something.

I inquired as to just what he thought I could do that he wasn't or couldn't. It was at this point in the conversation that I heard about me being in a 'special' position in the university. According to this professor, I was seen as something akin to Jerry Lewis and HIS KIDS. Whoa, wait a minute. I said I thought that Jerry was probably a fine human big, but these were not MY KIDS. My friend persisted that I was the one person to perform this transformation or metamorphosis. I had the power.

This was not the first time this kind of situation had happened. A few years earlier a local policeman had come up in the stands at one of our men's basketball games to inform me, that one of my kids were stranded out on the shoulder of the road on Route 23 to Cottonwood. I recommended that he or someone should go and 'undstrand' them—just like a regular person. It turned out this fine young man was stinking drunk and at sometime in the night decided to go visit a friend up in Cottonwood, some thirteen miles from Marshall. This is not too bad, but given he was a quadriplegic and in an electric wheelchair added a most interesting aspect. It also seems that no one really took him seriously and all his buddies went to bed. But our little hero was off and running. I never found out the true sequencing of the trek, but somehow he made it up the highway within three or four miles to his destination before disaster overtook him and he dumped out of his chair. Some motorist spotted him and, viola, go get good old Lew Shaver to the rescue. There was a positive end, although a terrible hangover, to the situation. Another motorist, in a van, stopped at the scene, loaded him and his chair into the van and returned him back to the university dorm.

I do think I can speak from a position of strength that not many of my players over the years would really want me as their parent, guardian, and certainly not their nanny or savior.

I related this story to my professor friend and assured my esteemed colleague that I indeed would speak to the young man and work my magic. But walking on water was a bit beyond me. But Jerry and I have a lot in common—right?

Armed with this mandate or maybe just reminded about what some of the primary objectives of our program was—to get people going—using athletics as part of this effort, I did call Dick and asked him to set up an appointment to talk. He accepted. The rest is history. I have no idea of why and probably should refrain from attempting to be too psychological. It happened.

His sophomore year was dramatic in the difference. Hey, maybe there was some magic. And if anyone wants to believe this I have a bridge or two to sell them.

Of all the people and players I asked to share with me what it meant to be a Bronco, to be treated as an athlete, Dick's response is truly one of the most significant in my opinion.

I have very little insight what turned the corner for him. I only know he turned and became a dear friend to this day. Even the discussion about his first few months with Southwest troubles me. Who am I to judge and label him a 'closet' anything? Perhaps it was his way to process and to determine the appropriateness involved with his participation. His response, his words are one example of an individual who, 'walked the walk.' He wrote:

As a prologue, I started this endeavor attempting to keep this retrospective of the Broncos on an objective, dispassionate plane, but I found myself relating to the Broncos on a very personal level. I guess that must have been trying to tell me something...

The Bronco environment represented a radically different approach towards the handling and 'treatment' of disabled students. The traditional (and still all too pervasive) approach is to employ the 'rehab' concept of dealing with the disabled. By that I mean that the person is looked upon as disabled (or even crippled) first, and a person (student) second. The possibility of that person being an athlete doesn't even figure in the formula. Even now, the idea that someone with a disability could be a top athlete is seldom taken that someone with a disability could be a top athlete is seldom taken seriously. The Broncos, on the other hand, looked upon the individual as a student/athlete who also happens to have a disability. This can be a very subtle difference on the surface, but can mean a large difference in how that individual perceives themselves and how they are perceived by others. It is a very important piece of the 'rehabilitation' equation that the disabled person not only finds peace, acceptance, and equality within themselves, but also that the 'able-bodied' population recognizes and acknowledges that comfort level!

To that end, there are four major concepts that come to my mind when talking of the impact of the Bronco program: Independence, Confidence, Self-Esteem, and Dignity.

The traditional approach of rehabilitation seemed to tacitly emphasize what your limitations were and what you couldn't do. "You can't do this, you can't do that, blah, blah, blah." It is really amazing the kinds of insidious 'head trips' (i.e. limitations) society can lay on the overall public consciousness, as well as each one of us individually. I can remember distinctly when the first artificial heart transplant (with Barney Clark I believe) was in progress and the hospital spokesman was making a statement in regard to the prognosis of Clark once he was able to leave the hospital and live on his own. The spokesman was explaining to the assembled reporters how easily Clark would be able to get around even though he would be attached to a machine placed on a cart, which would be driving his artificial heart. He said Clark would be "quite mobile—certainly more mobile than a paraplegic." That just about blew my mind! Here was a spokesman for a major hospital telling the WORLD that this guy attached to a 300-pound machine was going to be more mobile than me! Fortunately I already knew better, but its no wonder there are so many misconceptions about the disabled and their capabilities when the so called experts can't even get it right...

With the Broncos, while person's physical limitations were recognized (you certainly can't ignore them), the emphasis was on how to get around those limitations. What other options were there available to accomplish what you want to accomplish? How can we use our perfectly functional brain to figure out some alternatives? Because this atmosphere was present, a person discovers that they could indeed enjoy a relatively independent life-style after some 'trial and error' and a little help from our friends (we knew who those able bodied people were good for something anyway!!). The mindset that you were doomed to a 'nursing home' type setting was convincingly dispelled.

The Broncos as a group helped each other, 'comparing notes' concerning how to handle problems that inevitably come up when you are dealing with a bunch of wheelchair users in a relatively inaccessible world. The big thing about learning how to overcome these problems was not that it was so unique in a 'generic' sense, any rehab unit shows you how to transfer to your chair from bed, or dress yourself, etc., as a Bronco you had to figure out how to get in your chair from the floor after you tipped over during a basketball game, or how to get in a van which was four feet off the ground. These problems WERE unique!! Those were the ones, which really prepared you for the real world. It is an unfortunate fact of life that the world is very inaccessible!! Once you have dealt with these problems, the every day problems are a piece of cake.

So far, I've dealt mostly with the 'socialization issues' of the Broncos. Obviously that was and is an important part of the Bronco package, but the bottom line of the Broncos is the competitive sports aspect of them. We've all read and heard the clichés of how sports 'builds character,' develops a 'teamwork attitude,' instills a 'sense of discipline,' etc. While that can be true, more often than not those issues have become lost in the shuffle, as money, greed, and self-importance have come to the forefront. The Broncos remain one of the few 'pure' sports entities where those long lost qualities and virtues still ring true. There is no big (or even small) money involved, no cars, giveaways; large adoring crowds etc., to taint of spoil what it is all about. What was there was the chance to realize what is within yourself. It has been said that sports reflect life and all that is engendered in the 'human condition.' The Broncos gave a person the opportunity to participate in sports (and thereby life) and take it of whatever level you wanted, whether just for the sheer enjoyment of it, or maximum competitiveness (or both!). Through the Broncos I was able to travel to other cities, meet new people, and enjoy the camaraderie of a 'team', which embodied that which sports should be. As time has gone by, the start the Broncos gave me has enabled me to travel and compete all over the United States as well as a couple of foreign countries. This has in turn greatly affected my participation in life as a whole, whether just for the pure enjoyment of it or 'maximum competitiveness.'

I guess throughout my career as a Bronco, I began to notice that there was a difference between those disabled people who were involved with the Broncos, and those who weren't. It seemed that many of those who weren't involved tended to be (certainly not everyone of course) a little less adventurous and maybe even a little more bitter about how their life turned out. I can recall some people who always seemed to carry a chip on their shoulder and I thought that they probably would never totally come to terms with themselves and find their own peace. Some were never able to find the level of self-esteem they needed. I strongly believe that the people coming out of the Bronco program maintained a much better attitude than those who were not involved. From that attitude about themselves came the level of self-esteem that we all want to get.

All of these types of programs be it the Broncos or all those 'help groups' such as AA, are all trying to help people find something important—dignity. The

Broncos took a unique approach towards that goal, enabling you to come to terms with yourself, to find peace within yourself so you can concentrate on your personal goals and achievements just as you would as an able-bodies person. To me, finding the dignity that was stripped away from me in that awful instant (my accident) was the final step to achieve before I could move on...

Anyway, I want to finish this treatise with a little anecdote. It was one privately momentous occasion, which meant a lot to me and really demonstrated what participating in the Broncos can do. My track and field teammates and myself were flying from Minneapolis to Honolulu, Hawaii for the national track and field meet there. As we were flying over the Pacific, a bunch of us were talking and having a great time looking forward to getting to the 'island paradise.' I was sitting there enjoying the moment when I realized that that day just happened to be the ninth anniversary of my accident!! I thought it was incredible that here I was on my way to Hawaii just like some 'normal' person, contrasting it to what I thought my life would be in those dark days and months after my injury. To me that was what the Broncos represented—getting 'back to normal'!!!!

Concluding Remarks

This has been a sharing of feelings and experiences spent in timeless hours in a gym, of thousands of miles traveling all over the United States and beyond, of practices and games, and of days and nights spent together.

The words were mine told as a result of my experiences with those who lived and shared with me a unique lifestyle. It is basically the story of those who lived it; nothing more, nothing less. Being my narrative, as I remembered it, any mistakes, misinterpretations, lack of accuracy and any distortions were mine. I take sole responsibility for the telling. I kept the research to a minimum, believing the true story was what I remembered not what exhausting research would produce to impress anyone.

Therefore, the narrative was mine as I could reconstruct in my own style. Some stories were composites, a combination of events or individuals. In gathering information and material for the book, over a period of some ten to fifteen years, I asked former players to write me a paragraph, page or so indicating what it meant to them to be involved in our program.

What do I think any of this means? I sure would like to offer something profound like the Golden Rule, "Do unto others as you would have them do unto you." I'm not sure. I know it was unique. Over the past few years I have been approached by many people who mentioned that I lived the career that they would love to have for themselves. In retrospect, maybe it is just that simple. It happened and it was good.

I closed the scrapbook and began to gaze around the walls where all my treasured plaques, awards, and of course the pictures of past glories hung. Don't get me wrong, I'm proud of the awards from the students and the pictures of past teams and past championships and…And, anyway lots of memories. Maybe too many. My education, albeit politically incorrect, was amazing and to this day continues to be.

0-595-29254-2

Printed in the United States
47050LVS00003B/282